MIRACLE IN MOSTAR

GERARD KELLY lives in Paris with his family and is seconded from British Youth For Christ to an inner-city church. He has a previously published book of poetry called *Rebel without Applause*.

LOWELL SHEPPARD is National Director of British Youth For Christ and is on the Spring Harvest Executive. Lowell has previously written, with Catherine Butcher, *Never Ending Adventure*.

This book is dedicated to the people of Mostar,
and in particular
to Viktorija Skrinjaric and Jasmina Dedic.
Born into war, may you grow to be children of peace.

Miracle in Mostar

Gerard Kelly and Lowell Sheppard

A LION BOOK

Published by
Lion Publishing plc
Sandy Lane West, Oxford, England
ISBN 0 7459 3302 5
Albatross Books Pty Ltd
PO Box 320, Sutherland, NSW 2232, Australia
ISBN 0 7324 1237 4

First edition 1995
10 9 8 7 6 5 4 3 2 1 0

A catalogue record for this book is available
from the British Library

Printed and bound in Great Britain
by Cox & Wyman Ltd, Reading

Contents

	Authors' Note	6
1	Devil's Fingers, Angel's Wings	11
2	Three Men and a Baby	21
3	My Way, My Truth, My Life	33
4	A God Called 'Abba'	45
5	A Church is Born	56
6	Balkan Beirut	82
7	A Friendship Like *Melem*	94
8	Mostar, *Moj Grad*	107
9	Bridge Keepers of Mostar	120
10	Jasmina's Story	133
11	Hope for the World	146

Authors' Note

We first visited the former Republic of Yugoslavia in November 1992, as part of a delegation from Spring Harvest. We were unaware, at that time, of the story which would later unfold, linking Mostar and Rijeka in a chain of hope. As we observed the developments in Mostar, and as we subsequently researched this book, interviewing the participants in depth, our conviction was strengthened that this is a story which must be told. It is not finished yet, by any means. At the time of writing, Bosnia is still not at peace; in Mostar, Croats and Muslims are not, at this moment, killing each other, but the Bosnian Serb forces remain entrenched in the surrounding hills, their heavy artillery menacing the city. Shells are occasionally fired. Only God knows what the future holds for Mostar, but there is, at the heart of the Neretva valley, a haven of reconciliation and peace. Something extraordinary has happened in Mostar.

Although we have been involved personally, we have chosen not to write ourselves into the book, preferring to focus on the people at the heart of the story. We have both been deeply affected by our contacts in Croatia and Bosnia. Stevo Dereta, Nikola and Sandra Skrinjaric and others like them have challenged and encouraged us. Their bold faith is an inspiration to our own. We consider it a privilege to know them, and in some measure to have shared in their lives.

In putting the book together, Lowell has concentrated on interviews and research, Gerard on writing. We have worked together on shaping and developing the overall story-line; and despite not including ourselves in the narrative, the views we have expressed about the events in Mostar are very much our own.

There are many people we wish to thank:

in Bosnia: Klaus Domke, Karmelo and Ivon Kresonja, Ljerka Simunkovic, and all the members of the Mostar evangelical church;

in Croatia: Stevo and Jadranka Dereta, Peter and Lidija Mackenzie, Ladislav and Melanija Ruzicka, Teo Secen, Vesna Vuletic and the staff of the Life Centre in Crikvenica, and the people of Camp Hidroelektra at Ucka;

in Austria: Dennis Banker;

in the United Kingdom: Wendy Beech, Dennis Birch, Paul and Sue Brooks, Kris Calver, Graham Dale, Frances Grant, Andy and Helen Harrington, Chrissie Kelly, Judy Lloyd, Maurice Lyon, Charlie Lockyer, James Loring, Claire Price, Chris Seaton, Helen Share, Kande Sheppard, TVB, the leadership and staff of Spring Harvest, Youth for Christ and the trustees and management team of Novi Most;

in the United States: Mark Jevert and Larry Russell;

We wish especially to thank Nikola and Sandra Skrinjaric in Mostar for their hospitality, refreshing honesty and inspirational perseverance.

Gerard Kelly
Lowell Sheppard
OCTOBER 1994

The Bosnian region of former Yugoslavia

The Centre of Mostar

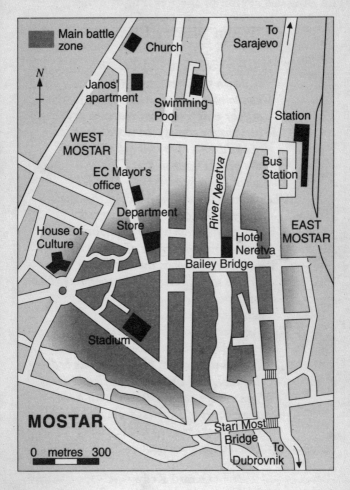

Main battle zone

N

Church

To Sarajevo

Janos' apartment

Swimming Pool

WEST MOSTAR

Station

EC Mayor's office

Bus Station

Department Store

EAST MOSTAR

House of Culture

Hotel Neretva

River Neretva

Bailey Bridge

Stadium

MOSTAR

0   metres   300

Stari Most Bridge

To Dubrovnik

When Winter Comes

When winter comes, an icy breath
    of death will blow across this sky.
  When winter comes, the gripping frost
    of fear will freeze the tears we cry.
  When winter comes, the wordless voice
    of children's eyes will ask us why
    the people have to die,
    when winter comes.
When winter comes, the bones of the dead
    will fill this aching city's streets.
  When winter comes, our trembling hands
    will clutch the scraps of food we eat.
  When winter comes, the 'cleansing'
    of this sorry place will be complete,
    as hope concedes defeat,
    when winter comes.
When winter comes, the last few bags
    of bartered rice will be no more.
  When winter comes, we'll burn our beds
    for fuel, and shiver on the floor.
  When winter comes, no keys will keep
    the wolves of sickness from our door:
    we'll be the wasted lives of war,
    when winter comes.

Gerard Kelly

1
Devil's Fingers, Angel's Wings

What is a gun for?
A gun is for making things.
What does it make?
Orphans, widows,
Grief.

Steve Turner, 'Gun', from *The King of Twist*

MOSTAR, SEPTEMBER 1994

An autumn sun washed over the city of Mostar, keeping its temperature high, although it was certainly cooler than in the long, hot months of summer. The mountains, rising like grey-green walls on every side, held back the winds from all but the highest buildings, and the city had an air of stagnant isolation. It was easy to feel cut off in Mostar, even without knowing that the same mountains hid the barrels of a dozen or more artillery units. The guns were quiet, for the moment, but their sights were still trained towards the city.

From the widest avenues through to the narrow alleys and squares that marked off the residential areas, the streets of this 'jewel of the south' were littered with debris. Lining the pavements were old cars with their wheels removed, domestic rubbish, bricks and iron and pieces of building. The remnants of shell and bullet casings lay in amongst the rubble and, in places, skips left at the roadside had been converted into perpetual incinerators: modern day Gehennas whose flame was never quenched and whose strange scent hung, day and night, in the air.

Mostar was waking slowly from a three-year nightmare of war. Damage seemed to spread out from the centre like ripples from a splash. The buildings on the banks of the

Neretva river, which cut right through the heart of the city, had been utterly destroyed: their broken walls, twisted metal and fallen stone were like the setting in some tasteless video-arcade game. Further out, the damage was less extreme, but it was evident at every turn. Every wall was pock-marked by bullets and shrapnel, and many surfaces were more seriously holed by artillery shells. On some, the animated spray-pattern of mortars was marked so clearly that you could still picture the moment of impact. The running for cover, the screaming, the rush to find help for the wounded—these were over, at least for the time being; but it was easy, from the graphic images left behind, to reconstruct the scene. The number of bullet holes must have run to millions—in walls, lamp-posts, road signs and cars—and the simple fact was that living human beings, as much as these inanimate things, had been on the receiving end of this hot-metal assault.

An uneasy peace had settled on the city. The Washington Accord, signed in February 1994, re-created a Croat–Muslim Federation, and prepared the ground for a long-term settlement. The subsequent demilitarization of the city in July brought further change, consolidated by the European Union (EU) appointment of the German, Hans Koschnick, as mayor. By the end of the summer, Mostar's people had begun to believe that peace really had arrived, though no one was yet making claims for its permanence. The front line area had become an eerie no man's land, patrolled by mixed units of different armies—made up of the same people who, until a few weeks before, had been killing each other. From time to time, shelling and automatic fire—both in the city and in the surrounding hills—still disturbed the fragile peace; but these were isolated incidents. For the moment, at least, the wild violence that had run like a torrent through Mostar had calmed.

In the midst of this cocktail of relief and tension, in which the hope of peace cohabited with the memory of war, Nikola Skrinjaric prepared to visit the eastern part of the city he called home for the first time since March 1993. He and his companions had arrived at the crossroads known as the 'Hit' checkpoint, named after the large department store which used to be there and by then distinguished only by a simple garden shed assembled to form a guardhouse. The 'Hit' checkpoint sat at the exact mid-point between the city's east and west: it was the 'Checkpoint Charlie' of Mostar.

Two hundred metres west of the shed, a broken table by the roadside represented the Croatian checkpoint that Nikola's group had already passed through. Three guards, in their grey-blue fatigues, were now sitting nonchalantly watching nothing happen, while a stray dog found shelter under their table. In front of them, a construction of sandbags, old furniture and debris blocked the road. Until very recently, this had been the border of Croat-controlled Mostar, the point beyond which no unarmed person would dare to go. There were no snipers now, neither at the barricade nor in the buildings around: but these had been, until July, their streets.

To the east of the shed, the checkpoint of the Bosnian army mirrored its western counterpart: another broken table, this time with an old armchair for company, the guards different only in their dark green uniforms which had a yellow thunderflash emblazoned on each arm.

Inside the shed itself, Nikola knew that the joint Croat–Muslim guard detail would be sitting at a table, checking the list of names of those authorized to cross the city. Civilians passing from east to west, or vice versa, had to apply twenty-four hours in advance for permission to make their journeys, so that lists of names could be copied to each of the three checkpoints—the west, the mid-point and the east. More heavily-armed United Nations (UN) troops watched from the sidelines with uneasy indifference. Around the hotel which was now both home and office to the EU-appointed mayor, there were more UN troops in sight, and here they were more alert. Just two weeks previously, a bazooka attack had burnt out the office of the mayor, sending a tremor not only through the city, but through the international community. Had he been killed, the fragile peace could very easily have shattered.

Nikola entered the shed nervously. He had no love of guns, and was always alert and polite in the presence of the militia. He knew not only that these men had been fighting until very recently, in front line positions, but also that they had been fighting each other. He and his companions were not included on the list of names, but had, instead, special passes.

'Why are you visiting east Mostar?' asked the senior member of the Croat contingent. In the Bosnian armed forces, a senior member was usually older than twenty-two; an alarming proportion of the men who had fought, and died, had been younger.

'We are with a humanitarian agency,' Nikola replied.

Earlier on, he had worn his clerical collar when applying for the pass. Roman Catholic priests still commanded a strong respect among Croats, and the tiny number of ordained ministers who were Protestant were afforded the same privileges. Later, Nikola had changed back into a T-shirt, fearing the impact that a Christian 'uniform' might have in the eastern part of the city. Each of Nikola's three roles was represented by a different identity card; he was the ordained leader of the Mostar evangelical church, and he was also the director, for Bosnia-Hercegovina, of the Agape aid agency. Which card to show to whom was sometimes a delicate choice.

'OK', the guard muttered, handing back the pass and the small collection of passports. Nikola and his companions turned towards the river, and he took his first steps in sixteen months into east Mostar.

East Mostar was the area that had remained under the control of the Bosnian army and it included much of the former city centre and all of the old town. To the west, the graffiti wars had left many buildings tattooed with the red-and-white chequered shield of Croatia, the single most potent symbol of national identity: in the east the same was true of the yellow-on-blue lilies of Bosnia-Hercegovina. But this was not the only difference. While the two sides had suffered fairly equal losses in the sniper wars, this had not been the case in the war of the big guns. The east had been pounded, levelled and pounded again. The result was a scene of utter devastation.

By September 1994, a staggering area, perhaps two-thirds of the city centre, had been destroyed. The buildings still standing were in a state of complete dereliction. Remaining structures had been looted, so that only the twisted, tumbling skeletons of the buildings remained. Some of them now served as unofficial rubbish dumps, with domestic garbage piled on top of the rubble. The 'Hit' department store, the great block at the very heart of Mostar that had been the pride of the Communist regime, was a charred silhouette. The formerly prestigious Hotel Ruza, a mausoleum of plaster and marble, was a broken shell, and a sign welcoming tourists to Yugoslavia was peppered with bullet holes. A ten-storey bank, visible from many points in the city and at the centre of the front line, was a tattered frame, every one of the glass and perspex panels of its walls shattered.

Just a hundred metres from the bank, beyond the Hit checkpoint, a Bailey bridge had been installed, donated by the British Overseas Development Agency. Opened on 12 September, it provided the city's only vehicle crossing-point over the steep Neretva valley, formerly spanned by the seven bridges of Mostar. Its freshly painted green metal sides and brass plaque declaring it a gift from Britain to all the people of Mostar had a strange newness in the midst of such destruction. Most of the buildings for a hundred metres either side of the checkpoints were deserted. In the past eighteen months these had been among the most dangerous streets in the former Yugoslavia—by implication, in the world. Even if peace were to hold, it would be weeks or months before people and businesses had the courage to move back in. Even then, they would not, at first, be coming to live or work, but to build.

The old city began a block or so into east Mostar itself, and here there were more signs of life, with people crowding the narrow streets. In the gutters, makeshift cardboard-box tables served to offer, for sale or barter, tiny collections of anything saleable, from cigarettes and old cabbages to shoes and soap. A temporary system of piping brought water to central standpipes, to which a steady flow of people came with plastic containers. Some saved their energies simply by bringing their washing up into the street, or drinking directly from the pipes. One or two offices were open, mostly for aid agencies or government departments, and a few small shops were doing business. But life for the most part took place in the streets, where broken stone and twisted metal were the backdrop. The atmosphere, despite all this, was almost casual: there was a shared sense of relief that firing of shells and bullets had stopped. A city which had held its breath for months was finally breathing out again.

The market place had reopened and beyond it, towards the site of the old Stari Most bridge, even one or two souvenir stalls were operating: selling to a trickle of foreigners, many of whom represented aid agencies or the press. Their wares were displayed in doorways, on makeshift shelves and tables. Mementos of old Mostar, retrieved or looted from pre-war storerooms, sat alongside the newer souvenirs— bullet and shell casings pulled out of the rubble, paintings of the Stari Most, wooden Mostar plates and Turkish-style crockery; there was even a portrait of Tito available. On a stall at a former prime site overlooking the Neretva, 1980s guidebooks in five languages still offered the Communist version of Mostar's history, in which Tito shared centre stage with 'The Working Peoples of Yugoslavia'.

Until 1991, these streets had been a tourist bottleneck, funnelling crowds from around the world into the tiny span of the Stari Most, remnant of the Ottoman past and symbol of the city. It was from the guards who patrolled these river banks four centuries ago, the Mostari, that the city derived its name. The Stari Most bridge was the one landmark of

Mostar that no visitor could ignore, as central to the identity of the town as the Eiffel Tower is to Paris. Because of the war, the narrow streets had become all but deserted, and the bridge itself was gone. The parapets still stood on each bank, like the stumps of amputated arms, and the viewing platform was still in place; but where once the elegance of sixteenth-century stone filled a million viewfinders, there now stretched only a cable-and-steel footbridge, carrying with it a single, fragile telephone line.

In his novel *The Bridge over the Drina*, Ivo Andric speaks, through the character of a nineteenth-century Muslim, of this legendary creation of Bosnia:

When Allah the Merciful and Compassionate first created this world, the earth was smooth and even as a finely engraved plate. That displeased the devil, who envied man this gift of God. And while the earth was still just as it had come from God's hands, damp and soft as unbaked clay, he stole up and scratched the face of God's earth with his nails, as much and as deeply as he could. Therefore ... deep rivers and ravines were formed which divided one district from another, and kept men apart ... And Allah felt pity when he saw what the Accursed One had done ... so he sent his angels to ... spread their wings above those places and ... men learnt from the angels of God how to build bridges; and therefore, after fountains, the greatest blessing is to build a bridge, and the greatest sin is to interfere with it.

If ever a river could be said to have been gouged by the devil to divide one district from another, it is the Neretva, with its deeply carved gorge cutting through the very heart of Mostar. If ever a bridge could have been likened to the wings of angels, it would have been the Stari Most, symbol of the city. It had survived four centuries of war, invasion and earthquake, of footfalls of tourists in their millions. Graceful as a ballerina, elegant as lace, it was this old bridge which had given Mostar its name and spanned its cultural diversity. When war carved the city crudely into two, and every other bridge was down, it became a slender icon of hope, a bridge between two worlds. Most of the people of Mostar, and many further afield, know exactly where they were when they heard that the Stari Most had fallen. Like the shooting of Kennedy or the death of Elvis, the tumbling of these ancient stones into the swirling Neretva sent shock waves around the world.

Mostar was, once more, a divided city. The few people who made the crossing from east to west, or vice versa, knew that for the time being they were moving between two cities. No one was allowed to stay on 'the wrong side' for more than three days. Most, therefore, remained reluctant to cross, afraid of being trapped. Nevertheless, there had been a consistent flow of people from one side to the other which had left two populations dominated by two distinct ethnic groups: Croats in the west and Muslims in the east. The separation was not total, and could never be: both groups still contained ethnic minorities—some in mixed marriages, some simply refusing to allow their loyalty to their home town of Mostar to be split. But on both sides, nationalist sentiment had tried its best to stamp its own distinct character. For over 400 years, this city had been the meeting point of east and west, of Islam and Christianity. President Tito, who saw both as culture and neither as faith, did all he could to make the city a melting-pot, to create a single, mixed culture. The old tourist guidebooks write proudly of monuments from Roman Catholic, Orthodox and Muslim cultures; but even more proudly of the new socialism which, from the liberation of 1941 onwards, worked to supersede all three. Just three years of divergence, war, and violent ethnic 'cleansing', along with a soft variety that continues today, swallowed fifty years of blending together. The Neretva valley became, once again, the dividing line between west and east. In one or two isolated pockets, a tiny effort towards rebuilding had begun. In the main shopping street of east Mostar there was, for the first time in many months, the sound of hammers. But for the most part, the process of reconstruction needed to wait until peace had proved permanent. No one wanted to replace windows only to see them blown out again. For the time being, derelict buildings remained deserted, roadblocks unmoved, and border patrols armed. And on both sides, the bereaved counted, many in double figures, their lost relatives.

For Nikola, the sight of east Mostar and its deterioration since he first saw it, on 20 March 1993, served to reinforce the horror that the city had lived through. For sixteen months, these streets had been out of bounds to him, and news received across the divide had been infrequent and sketchy, too often coloured by the interests of one or other power group. Walking through this deserted battlefield, it was as though the very heart of the place had been torn out: every human activity associated with the life of a city had been pushed out to make room for killing. War had been the master of these streets. Nikola wondered what it would take, what depth of change in human hearts, to reassert the rule of peace.

He held in his hand a note scribbled with the name and address of a Muslim friend, Alesa. Kept in a Croat prison for three months in 1993, Alesa had been smuggled a copy of Billy Graham's *Peace With God*, and had been deeply affected by what he read. On his release, he had been able, for just three weeks, to join the Mostar church, finding in it new friends and new hope. But a wave of ethnic 'cleansing' had carried him, like many others, to the east. Twice the church had been able to send food parcels, through the Red Cross, but then all contact had been lost. Just twenty-four hours beforehand, Nikola had heard that Alesa was alive and safe, and that he had held to his Christian faith throughout the siege of east Mostar.

Nikola was anxious to make contact, and to give whatever help the church, and the aid programmes related to it, could offer. He knew that the church, which had been active in wartime, had equally a role to play in peace. Finding this one man, who for twelve months had been cut off from contact with the church, was part of that role: just as it had been part of that same role to offer strength and support to the Muslims who had remained in the west. Support, encouragement, strength and solidarity—above all else, the church in Mostar had stood for community.

Throughout the former Republic of Yugoslavia, through the years of war, ordinary people had suffered—and are still suffering—deep pain and anguish; and Nikola knew that those who were part of the evangelical church of Mostar had suffered neither more nor less than their neighbours. The difference, for them, was that in their suffering God had met with them: that in their dark night of war, faith had become a living flame. This was the miracle of Mostar: that in the deepest valley, black with the very shadows of death, a stream of hope could be found.

Nikola remembered the first time he had walked these streets: alone, afraid and a long way from home. A reluctant recruit to the ranks of the brave, he had never felt more desperate than in his first hours in this city. Twenty-one months later, it was the place that he calls home. In between, it had more than once been the place of his near-death. Once, he had walked away from Mostar, saying he could not go back. But it had only been once. Like a rider on a raging bull, he held on to this terrifying city. Yet he would not be here at all but for a coded message sent by radio in the autumn of 1992: a cry for help, not from Mostar, but from its sister city, the bruised and broken Sarajevo.

2

Three Men and a Baby

Never have I witnessed such an eerie scene.
Broad daylight in a capital city and there is
not a soul on the streets. Newspaper skips in the
wind. This is not Sarajevo—this is the
Twilight Zone, and it is real.

Misha Glenny, *The Fall of Yugoslavia*

'Who is my neighbour?'

A first-century lawyer, the Gospel of Luke 10:29

ZAGREB, OCTOBER 1992

Peter Mackenzie read twice through his own scribbled note, hastily taken down from a phone call. A radio ham had picked up the coded message from Sarajevo which was to be passed to the Baptists in Croatia. It contained exactly the news for which Peter had been waiting, news which would take him south—out of Zagreb to the besieged and broken city of Sarajevo.

In seventeen years as a missionary in Yugoslavia, Peter, from Britain, had seen both discouragement and encouragement, both progress and set-backs. One of the encouragements had been the speed at which a new Baptist church had taken root in Sarajevo. In recent years, it had begun to flourish due to the efforts of Boris Kacarevic, by ancestry a Serb, who had moved to the city four years earlier with his Muslim-Montenegrin wife Senija and their three daughters. Within a few months, Boris and Senija had a group of forty people regularly meeting together, and a place to meet. Any satisfaction in such progress, however, was soon swallowed up by the larger, and more painful events of war.

When fighting broke out in Sarajevo, Boris and Senija had been very reluctant to leave either the church premises or its people. But they knew that for the sake of their children, and with all useful work at an end, they should leave. A first coded message to Zagreb, in the summer of 1992, confirmed that they wanted to leave the city, if possible, and also bore the news that Senija was pregnant.

For Peter in Zagreb, the appeal for help initiated a concern which became an obsession. Every spare moment, every usable contact was directed towards applying for the papers to get the family out of Sarajevo. Unfortunately, no amount of appealing or badgering had moved the authorities to allow them to leave. But a second message, in November, brought better news: a secret one-for-one exchange between the Serbs and Muslims had enabled the family to leave the city. They had been driven, under the threat of gunfire, to the nearby village of Fojnica. They would wait there for transport north.

Peter's first instinct was to find a driver. He thought immediately of a friend from Zagreb, a professional driver who seemed keen to be involved in the church's work with refugees. Peter phoned him, explained the situation, and asked his friend if he would join him on the trip.

'You're crazy, Peter', came the reply. 'It's too dangerous. I could never make such a trip, I'm sorry.' It was only months later that Peter would find out just how guilty his friend Nikola had felt the instant he had put the phone down.

Peter's next two contacts were more responsive. Stevo Dereta and Ladislav Ruzicka were both Baptist pastors themselves, and Stevo, from Rijeka, had been a close and trusted friend through most of the years that Peter had been in Yugoslavia. The two had often worked together on evangelism and teaching projects, networking with churches right across Yugoslavia. In 1991, these networks had become channels for relief supplies for refugees, and partnership in mission had become partnership in aid. Stevo, formerly a mechanic, had skills which were to prove invaluable in the long drives across the chaos of Croatia and Bosnia. Ladislav, who pastored a church in Karlovac, was a man of courage and physical strength, and also an excellent driver. For three months, the building which housed both his church and his apartment was on the front line.

All three people had made the decision that their calling as Christian workers must now involve them in the practical expression of love to those in need. All three agreed that the message from Boris would require them to drive into Bosnia.

Their trip, in an old Sherpa minibus, took almost five days. It was impossible to drive directly from Zagreb to Sarajevo, since the route cut across the Krajina—the sweeping crescent of Croatian territory now occupied by the Serb-backed Yugoslav People's Army (JNA). The alternat-ive route was much longer: southwards, down the coast road to Split, detouring where necessary to stay clear of the front lines; and then eastwards, through Mostar, to Fojnica. In many places they had to branch off from the main roads, some sections of which came under almost constant shelling. They stopped in Mostar to offload food and blankets at the offices of Agape, a Christian agency, and to pick up a local guide who could get them safely to Fojnica. When they reached the village, they were greeted by a family not of five but of six. Just eight days before, Senija had given birth to her first son, in a hospital where babies are not washed because water is too precious and caesarean sections, when needed, are carried out by candlelight. It was a moment of intense emotion, not only for this family with their new baby, but also for the three people who came for them: it was their farthest foray yet into the horrific arena of the Bosnian war.

In Mostar, in particular, Peter, Stevo and Ladislav had been deeply affected by the level of need. The Pentecostal church, the only evangelical community in the area, had closed, its building burnt to the ground and its members dispersed in the first waves of refugees to leave the city.

Only one man, Miro Jovisic, had stayed on. At first, he merely planned to keep his apartment, while his wife and children were evacuated to Osijek. But as he stayed on alone in Mostar, he was overwhelmed by the need for aid, and sent a desperate plea for help to nearby churches. Agape, a humanitarian agency based with the Pentecostal churches in Osijek, was able to begin a flow of aid which in turn brought help from wider Christian sources. The flow of people coming to the new Agape office to ask for help was unending. Working entirely alone, Miro urgently needed people who could work with him on a medium- to long-term basis. Mostar's pre-war population of 120,000 had been reduced to 80,000, but it was now predominantly dependent on aid. Although there was no work to be had in the city, no one was being allowed to leave. Moreover, each of the ethnic groups was determined to keep up its population in the area. Miro asked Peter and Stevo directly for help, and so gave them the question that was to stay in their minds for weeks: 'Who should we send to help Miro?'

'It won't be easy,' Stevo said to Peter during the long drive north. Their rescue operation was complete, and their minibus was now emptied of blankets and filled with passengers. 'Everybody is trying to get out of Mostar. Who'd be willing to go back in?'

Unknown to Stevo, the answer to that question was already on its way, through a new and unexpected development. Stevo had often been asked to act as a contact point for mission teams coming into Croatia and Bosnia. He was used to welcoming teams from Britain, the United States and elsewhere. Though the needs he had seen in Bosnia filled his mind, he did not expect to connect this with the team from Britain he had been asked to meet just a few days later.

RIJEKA, NOVEMBER 1992

Nestling on a residential hillside, in the Adriatic port of Rijeka, was the Pizzeria Dionis. Like most of the region's restaurants, it was built for tourists and reflected the cut-price chic for which the area was once known. It had black, marble-topped tables, subdued lighting, a chrome-finished bar, and a sound system tuned to Italian Radio. Only the restaurant's prices, erased and pencilled over almost daily as inflation and food shortages made their mark, indicated that anything was wrong. Even in November 1992, months into the economic disaster sparked by the virtual implosion of the tourist industry, the Dionis was open, picking up what business it could from the journalists, television crews and off-duty soldiers for whom Rijeka, for all its shortages, was a welcome rest.

On the day arranged for the rendezvous, Stevo sat over lunch with his four British guests. They were holding a debriefing session after their four-day visit to Croatia. Outside, the Adriatic sky had broken open in a violent rainstorm, and torrents half a metre deep were rushing down through the steep, narrow streets. Street lights failed, flashed, and re-lit. Lightning tore the sky apart every two or three minutes. There was an all-out war in the heavens, and it matched the terrestrial storm raging over all the country.

Stevo stared out from the Dionis' warmly-lit interior to the cold, wet streets outside and to the chaos beyond. He had returned only a few days earlier from the trip to Mostar and Sarajevo, and he still struggled to deal with the images it conjured up for him.

'The winter can be cold in Bosnia', he said. 'People are going to die.'

An articulate man in his mid-forties, Stevo was a Serb living in Croatia and married to a Croat. He had always rejected the nationalism which had shaped the views of so many people in his country, and when he talked about it, he spoke as much with his eyes as with his voice, with a visible passion about the waking nightmare into which his country had descended. His analysis of the situation was clearly the product of a sharp mind; yet his heart was burdened by pain.

'The real war', he began, 'was fought before a single shot was fired. It was a war of words and hatred, fought through daily papers and television. It took just months for people who had lived at peace for forty years to learn to hate each other. They had no defence against the lies raining down on them. By 1991, it was too late. Such a force of mistrust and hate had been released that nothing could contain it. The guns are evil, but the hatred is more evil still.'

Protestants had always been a tiny minority in Yugoslavia, and the Baptists were a smaller group still. Their great strength, as Stevo saw it, was that they stood apart, by definition, from the three monolithic faiths of the region: Roman Catholicism, Islam, and Orthodoxy. With no vested interests in the success of any one of the main religious power groups, Stevo and his colleagues had been free to respond to human need openly and without prejudice. Their churches had never been aligned to any one nationality, and usually reflected a complex pattern of membership, with many mixed marriages.

However, when the former Republic of Yugoslavia began to shake itself to death, waking in the process the sleeping beasts of Balkan ethnicity, Stevo was among those church leaders who knew immediately that they must respond—not least to the desperate, physical needs of the victims of war. His trips into Bosnia had now marked him indelibly with a concern for all ethnic groups, including the Muslim population—who were set to lose most, perhaps everything, in the vicious scramble for land and power.

The city of Rijeka, like Karlovac and Zagreb, had a strategic position in the traffic of displacement: through it, the flood of refugees flowed northwards and the convoys of aid worked south. Rijeka was the principal port of the Adriatic coast, containing its largest shipyard, and it was spared the physical damage of war when a well-timed withdrawal of military personnel reduced its value as a target. But the emotional scars were visible all the same. Because the city nestles in the lee of mountains that sweep almost into the sea itself, it has a micro-climate which, at the time, made it a safe haven for refugees fleeing the ravages not only of war, but of winter. The evaporation of the tourist trade had already brought doom to the local economy. But the influx of over 50,000 refugees, by the autumn of 1992, had stretched the resources of this city of 180,000 to its limits.

By establishing an aid agency, Moj Bliznji ('My Neighbour'), the Baptist churches of Croatia had, in fact, been able to respond to the crushing needs following the outbreak of war.

As the crises deepened, the relief work, for Stevo, all but took over from the role of church leadership. A half-built engineering works, one of the many interrupted construction sites that littered the mountain-sides above the city, was donated as a makeshift warehouse, and now housed the truck-loads of aid coming in from Germany, Switzerland, the Netherlands, Britain and Italy. Everything from beds and wheelchairs to sweets, toiletries and vegetables was found a place at the warehouse, to be distributed through a network of churches and families. More than 2,000 families in Rijeka had made space in their homes for refugees, and for many, Moj Bliznji was the only source of the extra supplies needed.

Talking at the Dionis of his hopes and fears for the future, Stevo's face betrayed the depth of his feelings. He had seen enough of the refugee crisis to know that the makeshift camps and donations of food were fast becoming inadequate. And he had witnessed for too long the steady, unstoppable growth of hatred and hysteria.

'Something has been released among our people: an evil, a hatred, that will take years to repair', he said, staring again into the chaotic darkness of the sky. 'There are some people who will never, in their lifetime, overcome the pain and anger they have felt these last two years. And long after peace has come,' he added, 'even when the homes are rebuilt and the schools are reopened, we will be faced with the echoes of this hatred.'

Stevo believed that as much as anything, the church, at this time of crisis, should be a broker of forgiveness.

'People must find a new power,' he said, 'the power to forgive. Reconciliation won't work as long as it remains a theory. People need to see it, to give it arms and legs. We believe that this time is like a crucible for the church: when we must choose whether to play our part or not.'

In the context of a region torn apart by the most virulent hatred seen in Europe since the fall of the Third Reich, Stevo's words had significance and urgency. He had no doubt about the identity of the real enemy—the loathing and intolerance that had swept over the Balkans. Unless this enemy were faced, he argued, other battles won would be hollow victories.

Stevo spoke on—of the need to forgive, of overcoming ethnic hatred with unconditional acceptance, of the need for the young to find hope again, and of the scale of the inhumanity which was now beyond the most horrific imaginable.

It was inevitable, therefore, for the discussion in the Dionis to turn to practical responses. The team meeting with Stevo came as representatives of Spring Harvest, a British-based Christian teaching conference which is held at various sites every spring, attracting up to 80,000 people. Their objective was to locate a project for which Christian young people in Britain could raise funds and pray. What could young people living in peace do in the face of such need? If they could raise money, how best could it be used?

Stevo's answer was immediate and assured, spoken with the self-confidence of a man who has thought long and hard about what he wants.

'It is people that are needed,' he said, simply, 'people willing to dedicate more than months, a lifetime if necessary, to the rebuilding of tolerance and hope among the young of Yugoslavia. They need to help meet the immediate needs, for food and shelter, certainly, but they need to look, too, beyond the immediate, to the work of rebuilding and repair.'

Just as his gaze ranged beyond the squat, square rooftops of Rijeka to the very edge of the horizon beyond, so his passion saw beyond immediate needs to the long haul.

'These people, though,' he added, 'must be nationals, not foreigners coming in. We are glad of the workers who come from abroad, but it is time for our own people to respond. The church must raise up its own army of workers.'

There was no suggestion of rejecting the work of those who come from outside. But Stevo believed, with great clarity of vision, that the most important response would be that which came from within, and that the commitment of the indigenous church to action would carry a message which would be all the more poignant. Even as he spoke, Stevo had in mind a young couple he had recently been working with; and he thought, too, of Miro and his need for help.

'These are our neighbours who are suffering', he said. 'It is we who must respond.'

The British team accepted Stevo's proposition immediately, convinced both of his judgment and of his analysis of the situation. By the end of their meal, they had agreed to raise the funds for a two-year appointment, trusting Stevo to select the worker. Neither they, nor he, knew at this stage what a difference their decision would make to a city 500 kilometres further south.

Outside, the rain continued unabated, lashing the city. Inside, a handshake across the table of a fashionable pizzeria opened the way for one small ray of hope in a devastated landscape.

GENEVA, SWITZERLAND, DECEMBER 1992

A thousand kilometres from Rijeka, David Owen, Cyrus Vance and a collection of tense, discordant delegates discussed both the prospects for peace and the thousands of deaths that each deal in the war over territory might bring. Their words had the potential to shape the lives of millions— or of no one, if their brokering failed.

Closer to home, in Karlovac and Zagreb, officials of the Red Cross and United Nations High Commission for Refugees (UNHCR) negotiated the fate of hundreds of thousands of refugees. In a disused army barracks in Karlovac itself, despondent and emaciated people now released from prison camps waited to hear if any country, anywhere in the world, would offer them asylum. Their numbers grew weekly by the hundred; the offers from the world community came in by the dozen. Crude wooden barriers erected across a public square made it clear to them that their residence in Karlovac was to be temporary and limited: they were guests of the Red Cross, not of the government. In the interim, they were to wait: citizens of nowhere, wondering if they would ever find their families, all but certain that they would never go home.

MOSTAR, BOSNIA-HERCEGOVINA, DECEMBER 1992

In Mostar, Andelko Matinovic, director of the city's main orphanage, surveyed the ruins of thirty years' work. Through the window of his temporary office he could see, one kilometre away, the bombed-out silhouette of the home over which, until six months ago, he had charge. It was now an empty shell, 135 children lighter than in its former life.

Andelko's face was deeply lined, and his eyes were red from lack of sleep—he had cried often in recent weeks. All around the city of his birth and adult life, other buildings had been similarly destroyed, but nothing had the power to move him from this wrecked and deserted home. In it, within the possibilities of institutional care, he had taken on a fatherly role for 135 young people. They were scattered now, some in safe pockets of the former Yugoslavia, others abroad. Of some he knew the locations, but of others he had only the most fragile of news. From a few, letters had reached him; but nothing in their contents had served to reassure him:

physically, they were safer—but Mostar was their home. Anything of substance in the fragile security they had, as orphans, held on to, was linked to this city, to its buildings, and to its people. It was where they belonged, it was what they knew. And Mostar was an incomplete city, as empty as the empty shell he stared at, without them.

CAMP HIDROELEKTRA, DECEMBER 1992

At Ucka, just north of Rijeka, the abandoned, rotting huts of a 1970s' road workers' camp had become home to 400 Bosnian Muslims, 300 of them children. Grieving the loss of their families and homes, they had made the best of the cold water, the cement floors and the fact that there was only one toilet for every eighty people. Emir Mevic was sixteen; his father was dead and his brother was still fighting in Bosnia. He scratched the walls with images copied from American hard-rock sweatshirts—a skull with a dagger through its eye sockets, dripping blood, and the words 'hate' and 'death', etched underneath in English.

TURANJ, CROATIA, DECEMBER 1992

All along the razor sharp cease-fire lines separating Croatia from the self-proclaimed Serbian Republic of Krajina, UN troops from every continent were piling sandbags, diffusing mines, investigating cease-fire violations and wondering out loud, in the presence of the international press, why they were there. At Turanj, formerly a residential suburb of Karlovac but now a burnt-out and deserted tract of no man's land, the frontier itself was straddled by Brada Gojak High School. Its roof was open to the sky, and rain and snow soaked into the piles of books, papers, report cards and achievement certificates that the looters had left behind. An abandoned history book lay, urine-soaked, in the entrance hall, open at a profile of Gandhi: a lesson in peace, interrupted.

In Bosnia itself, deep inside the dark belly of war, the fighting went on. Besieged cities were bombarded and starved, families were ejected from their homes in the scourge of ethnic 'cleansing', and unidentified bodies lay, rain-soaked, in ditches.

It was hard to believe, against these settings, that the promise to find money to employ one person in the work of reconciliation and relief could really make a difference. Against the scale of the United Nations, of the peace process, and of the international relief operation, it seemed a small gesture. But in such darkness, even small gestures have meaning. And in that darkness, then, when people of violence and people of power, influence or prestige had succeeded only in deepening the chaos, it was just such a small gesture that mattered. It was a cup of water given to the dying. It was a small, smooth stone of love, well-aimed, and sent spinning to the forehead of the giant, war.

3

My Way, My Truth, My Life

*Costly grace is costly because it calls us to
follow, and is grace because it calls us to follow
Jesus Christ. It is costly because it costs a man
his life, and it is grace because it gives him the
only true life.*

Dietrich Bonhoeffer, *Cost of Discipleship*, chapter 1

Courage is grace under pressure

Attributed to Ernest Hemingway

MOSTAR, DECEMBER 1992

Nikola pulled the ten-ton truck to a halt on the steep hillside.
To his right, the forest stretched to the very edge of the road.
To his left, just as immediately, the hillside dropped away.
Below, stretched out across the valley like a child's toys
littering the nursery floor, lay the city of Mostar. Tired from
the lonely hours of driving, Nikola's fatigue was redoubled
by the tug of fear and apprehension that had been growing in
him the whole journey. Two days on the road had brought
him, through countless checkpoints, roadblocks and forced
detours, the 700 kilometres from Zagreb. All that remained
was the final checkpoint, and the three-kilometre descent
into the city itself.

The last three hours of driving—inland, across the
mountains from Split—had been the most desolate. For
long stretches, the road had passed through a barren,
sparsely-populated region of rocks and scrub. The terrain
itself would be bleak at the best of times, Nikola thought, but
it was even more so driving alone, on Christmas Day, into
war. The lifeless landscape, the half-built homes—some

abandoned when war broke out, others left unfinished on purpose to avoid property tax—offered nothing to break up the grey scene. In front of most houses, a large metal frame supported the vines that would offer a leafy terrace of shade in the spring and summer, and an abundance of grapes not long after. But in midwinter, the vines themselves looked dead and twisted, like strange, contorted limbs: as if this was the wrong time to be passing through the region.

In the town of Imotski, a few kilometres short of what was now the Croatian-Bosnian border, Nikola had first begun to see the remains of battle: a few scattered houses had been shelled and in places there were signs of bullet fire. The border itself had been a ramshackle affair of caravans, with steel girders serving to block the road. In the rush to break up what was then the Republic of Yugoslavia, the chaos of war had taken over before anyone could find the time or money to build border posts. In the event, it was the guns, and the guards' willingness to use them, that made each frontier crossing secure.

Nikola had been tense and nervous at every checkpoint, knowing that at any one of them he could be detained or turned back. Even in peacetime, armed guards inspire respect at such crossings; in the volatile conditions of a war beyond the control of any central authority, in which local militias and maverick commanders have taken the place of local government, they inspire a truly legitimate fear. Each time he waited for his papers to be checked, he would strain to listen to the conversations of the guards, to pick up what news he could about the section lying ahead. In some of the areas he drove through, he was within a few kilometres both of the front lines and of the borders of 'Krajina'.

Nikola's own home town in western Slavonija, Novi Varos, had been among the first to fall to JNA occupation in the summer of 1991. It lay six kilometres north of the Bosnian border, on the main road east from Zagreb, and what was left of the town after its Croatian residents had first fought and then fled now formed part of Krajina. The new republic had created its own flag and printed its own money, but it was unrecognized by the international community who looked on it as Serb-occupied Croatia. Nikola had already moved out of Novi Varos by the time the war came, and was established in Zagreb, working as a transport manager. He had tried, unsuccessfully, to persuade his parents to leave their home, but in time, they were forced to do so anyway. Nikola's mother had taken a place on a refugee bus which was travelling to the north, while his father had chosen instead to head for the front lines to fight.

By the time Nikola had tracked down his mother, twelve other members of his family had also come to Zagreb and become his house guests. His first close contact with the refugee problem, in the shape of his own relatives, showed him what it was to lose everything: to be driven, inch by inch, from the land that had been home for generations.

At the same time, through an Evangelical church in Zagreb and through his friendship with Peter Mackenzie, Nikola began to be involved in the wider issues of refugees and the work among the thousands who daily flooded into Zagreb. He was convinced that his place was to stay in the Croatian capital—so much so that he told close friends that he believed that God had protected him during the war by giving him a safe haven in Zagreb. When asked to drive a minibus to Sarajevo, he refused, saying that the trip would be too dangerous. But his conscience, from that moment, was troubled. Not long after, he met, at Peter's house, Senija Kacarevic and her children, recently rescued on that same Sarajevo trip. He was deeply affected by their descriptions of the situation in Bosnia. Without accepting, just yet, that his involvement would ever reach beyond Zagreb, he began to wonder what he might do to help.

The answer came in the form of a truck. Moj Bliznji, based in Rijeka and co-ordinated by Peter's close friend Stevo Dereta, had been given funds to buy a truck large enough to collect aid supplies from Switzerland and Germany and distribute them around northern Croatia and Bosnia. But they had no driver. Nikola, both qualified and experienced for such a task, volunteered. He met up with Stevo, and helped in the choice and purchase of the vehicle. He had not known Stevo well before this, having met him only once or twice, but they struck up an immediate friendship. Nikola was glad of the opportunity to serve and Moj Bliznji were glad of his availability—and his driving licence!

The act of volunteering complete, Nikola had no choice but to say 'yes' to the first proposed delivery: a consignment of stoves, destined for the city of Mostar. The supply of electricity had been cut in parts of the city, and many people, driven from their homes, were living in makeshift shelters. With winter already underway, there was a desperate need for heat. Nikola was not happy to be driving into an active war zone, but he accepted that the job needed doing. He duly collected the load of stoves, and headed south to Zadar on Christmas Eve, to spend the night there before journeying on to Split and then to Mostar on Christmas Day.

Nikola was surprised to find, as he began to drive, that his reluctance had all but evaporated. Somewhere between the refusal to drive to Sarajevo and the agreement to drive to Mostar, something had changed. It wasn't that he saw fewer dangers—the more he learned of Bosnia, the more dangerous it seemed—but he felt compelled to do something, and driving was what he knew best. He knew he had made the right choice, and now he only had the fear to contend with.

Spread out across the valley floor, Mostar was grey and cold in the winter light. A weak sun was slanting into the city, throwing dull lines across the trunks of the tower blocks. In the far distance, the mountains formed a mottled backdrop, topped as they were with snow and laced with mists; they looked like sleeping dinosaurs that even the war could not wake.

The edge of the city to the west began slowly, with squat, square houses, their red tiled roofs thinly spread across the wide, flat valley floor; then there came residential blocks, stumpy, uniform and grey; and finally there came the bold blocks of the city centre, squeezed into the valley's deepest point, as if into the plug hole of some huge bath.

From two or three points among those first houses, Nikola could see smoke rising, thick and insistent, in the centre of the city. It was impossible to tell its exact source, but dark, cancerous patches marked the walls of many buildings, and there were empty spaces where other buildings ought to have been.

Nikola shuddered to think that other people, too, were observing the city from similar hillside vantage points. Armed with binoculars, they would be taking in its shape and landscape, assessing damage as a measure of success: like children who had thrown stones and were waiting for the splash. They would be watching, observing changes, finding the perfect moment—and giving orders to fire. Hidden though they were by the trees and rocks, distant from him though they might be, he sensed that he was in the very presence of evil.

A city of a million postcards, Mostar was known, until 1992, as a citadel of gentle stone and calm beauty. In among the newer homes and offices, old Mostar was an architectural treasure-house, preserving the delicate beauty of the Ottoman Empire. Visitors from around the world had been drawn to this Venice without canals, this Paris of the Balkans. For its own people, it was place of tolerance and trust, a model of co-habitation. Even in the heady barbarity of the Second World War, when ethnic rivalry exploded throughout the Balkans into violence and murder, Mostar was more or less immune. Within the former Republic, the Hercegovina province was known for its ethnic harmony, with Mostar as its capital and crown.

However, the ethnic tensions that had been building up since 1990 suddenly exploded into war in April, 1992. The JNA fought at first in Mostar itself, but then withdrew to continue shelling from the surrounding hills. A victim of its own geography, Mostar suffered one of the fiercest batterings of the three years of Balkan conflict.

Nikola found his fear deepening as he descended the steep road into the city. The mountain walls seemed to close him in. He caught himself wondering if he would come out of the city alive. Beyond the noise of the truck's engine, straining to keep the descent slow and safe, the thump and thud of distant shelling could be heard. He had been told at a briefing in Rijeka that the city was in an actual state of bombardment—it was not just under the threat of shelling, but was experi-encing it daily. A partial cease-fire had been negotiated, and the explosions to be heard were infrequent and distant, but he knew that at any moment a heavier rain could resume. From this distance, each explosion died in seconds, as if its work were over. But he knew, too, from the damage he had already seen, that the impact itself was just the start. Up in the hills, it might only be a noise. Down there, in the target zone, it would mean shattered glass, falling masonry and beams, a blind panic in the run for cover, perhaps a flaming vehicle abandoned in the road. Only from a distance, or through the sanitizing filter of television, does war take on the majesty of ballet. Up close, it hurts, and smells of death.

By the time he was steering the heavy truck through the streets of the centre, Nikola was in a state of shock. He had been observing the destruction of the city played out like a silent film on each of the twin screens of the truck's windshield. There was almost no one in the streets. Those who had the heart to celebrate Christmas were doing so at home, behind closed doors; but the covertness of such festivity had the effect of adding to, rather than relieving, the eerie sense of being in a city in suspended animation. It was Nikola's first experience of concentrated destruction, of the desolation felt when shells have fallen repeatedly, for days, then weeks, then months, on the same few square kilometres of city. He drove on with an almost apocalyptic sense of doom, fed in part by his own fatigue. He felt utterly alone, and useless in the face of such horror. Even God, at that point, seemed far away.

Faith in God had become a central factor in Nikola's life some seven years earlier, though his spiritual quest went back much further. A chance meeting, in the late 1970s, with a theology student who was also a faith healer, had awakened his interest in the whole realm of spiritual power. He had begun to experiment, using a pendulum for divining and to investigate a basis for spiritual healing. He had discovered that he was adept at this, and before long he had been offering total strangers a health analysis just by looking at them. In 1980, he had taken a contract to work in Algiers, transporting prefabricated housing units for work teams laying a desert pipeline. There he had soon become popular within the small, closed community around the project, and had practised both healing and water divination with considerable success. By the time he had returned to Zagreb one year later, spiritual healing had become a part-time business, offering a significant source of income alongside his more normal work activities. He had expanded his activities until he could open a 'clinic', at first in Zagreb and later in an old house he had been able to buy in Slavonija, not far from his parents. Commuting between the two, he had been successful, popular, and financially secure.

But he had also been sincere in his spiritual search. He had come into the practice of healing because of a personal motivation to find truth and meaning, not to make money. In his own mind, he had been quite prepared to move on from it if his searching led elsewhere. And more and more, he had found that while his gifts offered something to others, they held little satisfaction for him.

Nikola had begun to travel to meet up with fellow searchers, others whose experiences he could compare with his own, who had gone further or deeper. All this time, he was influenced by friends within the Roman Catholic Church. Catholicism is deeply rooted in Croatia, and many of those who, from the 1960s onwards, moved towards Eastern mysticism and what became the New Age movement, still had strong ties with their Catholic faith. Some practised both simultaneously; others, like Nikola, were simply open to anything that offered a deeper, more meaningful experience.

In his searching, Nikola had been interested to hear about a series of evangelistic seminars being led by a priest. He had gone along to find about 800 people crowded into the church. The priest had spoken simply about the feeling of inner emptiness so often symptomatic of modern life—an outward display of success masking an inner hunger. Nikola had recognized this as a perfect description of his own condition, and had eagerly responded to the priest's appeal for converts. Kneeling at the front of the crowded church, he had been told to express, in his own words, what he felt he should say to this Jesus he had come to meet. He had found himself echoing the words of the Bible:

'From now on,' he prayed, 'you will be *my* way, *my* truth, *my* life.'

The priest had advised Nikola that leading an effective Christian life would mean abandoning his more glamorous, and suspect, spiritual activities. This Nikola had agreed to do, and had thrown himself enthusiastically into the study of the Bible. But before long, he had been drawn back into his healing practices which came to dominate his life once more. It was only some time later, through contact with the evangelical church, that he saw the need to make a more decisive break with the past, totally abandoning his interest in occult power.

At this point, however, Nikola's commitment to Christianity became his central motivation and interest. He became involved in the Pentecostal church in Zagreb, and began to develop gifts of leadership and service. Peter and Lidija Mackenzie became significant personal advisers, and it was when he accompanied Peter to help lead a seminar in Rijeka, on the New Age movement, that Nikola had first met Stevo Dereta.

Speaking later of this first meeting, Stevo said that he had found Nikola to be *plah*, a Croatian word meaning shy and simple, used of people who do not put themselves forward. And yet Stevo had seen a strength in Nikola, a very special sense of peace. He had felt from the very first that he could trust him.

Nikola had come full circle, from New Age searcher to practising Christian, convinced that the meaning of his life lay in the expression, somehow, of his new faith. He had become enthusiastic and committed in speaking to others of the changes that had taken place in his life, and he was equally committed in serving, in practical ways. Now, however, the strength Stevo saw in him had been put to the test, perhaps more dramatically than either, at the time, could have known.

Nikola succeeded in locating the delivery address he had been given—the office of Agape—but found no one there. Just across the street was the office of a Muslim aid agency, Merhamet. It didn't, at the time, seem odd that Pentecostal Christians and Muslims should house their aid depots in the same street, effectively serving the same community. Nevertheless, Nikola believed it could only be a matter of months before such proximity would become impossible, the stuff of fantasy. Leaving the truck in the deserted street, Nikola watched from the side of the road as figures emerged from the buildings around to take a closer look: eerie half-shadows barely visible in the gathering dusk. He had heard horror-stories of how easily things could be stolen in such situations, from the truck's cargo to its wheels. His pulse quickened. He went to the Merhamet office and phoned the Agape representative, Miro Jovisic, who came to find him. They moved the truck on to the forecourt of a petrol station, which already had an armed guard, ready to unload it the next day.

In all, Nikola was to spend six days in Mostar, leaving the city on New Year's Eve. Once the stoves were unloaded, there was another job for which the truck was ideal. The building used by Agape as both office and warehouse had been too small, and Agape had been offered the use of another, at the eastern edge of town. Throughout Christmas week, Nikola worked with Miro using the truck to transfer

41

the contents of the old building to the new one. This gave him not only a practical task into which to throw himself, but also an intensive time of learning and discovery, in which he saw the pitfalls, as well as the positive sides, of aid work.

There were some initial complications with some British people whose names had been given to Nikola as contacts in the city. They had established themselves in Mostar, using money given through Stevo Dereta and Moj Bliznji, and had promised to initiate not only emergency aid provision but also, in the longer term, a rebuilding programme. They had won the confidence of many, but Nikola felt at once that something was wrong. There were tensions between them and Miro which produced quite an argument about who should take responsibility for the stoves; and there was an extravagance in their lifestyle which was incongruous in a city under siege. Nikola spoke by telephone to Stevo and to Peter, asking them to investigate. He himself tried to find out what had become of the money Stevo had entrusted to them. Their response was angry and defensive. Their relationship with Moj Bliznji was broken off, and the stoves were entrusted to Miro. Shortly afterwards, they pulled out of Mostar.

If this conflict served to heighten Nikola's sense of apprehension, it also strengthened his resolve. Mostar was all but cut off from the outside world, and groups like Moj Bliznji had little or no control over the ultimate destination of the aid they sent into the city. To add to this, Nikola saw at first hand how desperately Miro needed help. Working alone, Miro was reliant on volunteers, literally gathered from the streets, to load and unload the trucks and to staff the warehouse; the result was a low degree of efficiency and a high incidence of theft. There was no one working alongside Miro who shared his commitment to Agape's work. The operation simply wasn't working very well.

It grieved Nikola, too, in this short stay, to find that no church meetings were taking place in the city. He was convinced that, alongside the provision of aid, there should be some form of gathering, so that the life of the church could be expressed and communicated in different ways. As a natural evangelist, he had been willing to accept that the church must act to meet immediate, physical needs—but he retained, alongside this, his belief in the building and growth of the church itself. A warehouse could serve the needs of the city in the short term; but a church, once established, could go on serving in the much longer term, and would form the nucleus of local people who could carry the load for Agape, Moj Bliznji and others. His first commitment was to evangelism—to the building, person by person, of the living church.

Nikola had no clear idea about how to respond to these concerns: he knew that there was a need to begin something new in the city, but didn't know what. The clearing of the old warehouse now left an ideal space for meetings, were they to start again, and the availability of the new warehouse meant that the work of Agape was ready to expand. The previous church had closed when it had lost both its buildings and its people, but here was an opportunity to start again.

Even without a clear plan in mind, Nikola could see that there were opportunities here to do *something*. When Miro asked him directly if he would be prepared to come back to Mostar to work full-time, he found he was within a breath of saying 'yes'. He had, after all, been reluctant to come to Mostar at all; yet found himself compelled to do so. He had arrived in a state of fear and panic, and had been overwhelmed by the shock of seeing a city ravaged by war; yet as the waves of shock receded, he saw more clearly, beneath the damage, the human need. He had been confused by the abuses and disorganization among the supposedly Christian British aid workers, finding indulgence where he had expected Christian heroism; yet the experience convinced him that workers with integrity could make all the difference. He had been disappointed to find that no Christians meetings were being held; yet he was excited by the prospect of a new start. It was as if he had approached Mostar thinking only of the sacrifice, the potential for loss.

Once in the city, he began to see its potential for joy. There was something wonderful, he thought, about being in a place where the worst that some people could do still did not extinguish the hopes of others. He had seen the cost; now he saw the grace.

Gradually, during those six days of work, prayer and observation, Nikola became convinced that he should consider moving, to work full-time in Mostar. There were two reasons, however, for not making such a commitment straight away. The first was that he had only just offered Stevo his services as a truck-driver. Nikola was coming to like Stevo not only as a friend, but also as a deeply respected pastor and adviser. Surely Stevo would judge him to be utterly irresponsible if he returned from his first delivery trip ready to hand in his notice? Nikola wanted to talk his feelings through with both Stevo and with Peter before making any decision. The second reason was more personal, and more pressing. If the trip to Mostar had happened just a few months earlier, Nikola would have been settling future choices for himself alone. But that was no longer true. The unfolding of events on a national and international scale through the months of 1992 had been matched by changes on a personal scale. By the time he had accepted the task of delivering stoves to Mostar, he was no longer free to make such a decision alone.

4

A God Called 'Abba'

Love has no enemies,
For it has never declared war.

Stewart Henderson, in *Homeland*

ZAGREB, DECEMBER 1992

Sandra Baljkas put the phone down, breathing deeply to compose her thoughts. The last three weeks had totally changed her perspective on the future. It was not just a question of preparing to live as a couple, but also of uprooting from Zagreb.

The plan had been to find a home in or near Rijeka, to be close to the Moj Bliznji offices and warehouse. Nikola would operate from there, going between the refugee camps, travelling into Germany and Switzerland, and occasionally journeying down into Bosnia. Sandra had already begun to get used to the idea of leaving Zagreb, her home for all but six of her twenty-six years. But this evening's phone call had set her life on end again: Mostar was different.

Nikola had poured out to her, above the crackle and fizz of a poor quality phone line, his convictions about all that was happening in Mostar, and about all that could happen.

'The conditions are terrible here', he had told her. 'Nearly half the city is destroyed. There are people here who are starving—the food they get from the humanitarian groups is all they have. I need to ask you, Sandra. What would you say if I said I was hoping to come and work here?'

'For how long?' Sandra had asked, unsure if he meant weeks, months or years.

'I don't know', said Nikola. 'For as long as I'm needed. Miro just can't do the job alone: he needs help.'

'If it's the right thing to do, you must do it', Sandra affirmed.

'But I also need to ask you', Nikola continued, nervously. 'Would you be prepared to live here too, to work together with me in this city?'

'Have you talked to Stevo, and Peter?'

'Not yet, not about coming down here to live. They know what the situation is here already. I know it must seem strange for you; it's such a big change of plan. But if you could just see the situation here, I know you would feel as I do.'

'I know that's true', said Sandra. She could hear in his voice, even over the phone, that he had been deeply touched by what he had seen of the city. She was learning to trust his feelings about such things.

'It's so much to think about,' she went on, 'but if it is right, then we should do it together.'

'What about this week?' Nikola said. 'Why don't you come down straight away, and spend the New Year down here?'

'I can't', Sandra replied. 'I have obligations at work, I can't just walk out. It's too quick: and this is a big decision. I think you should come back, as planned, and we'll talk then.'

Almost before her hand had released the phone, Sandra knew that she was turning a corner in her life. She knew that Nikola would not even mention the idea of working in Mostar unless he was convinced of it. He had experienced, in that city, something that had moved him deeply. Only weeks earlier he had been saying that he saw God's hand in keeping them in Zagreb, where they were safe. Even more recently, he had told her how crazy he thought Peter was to attempt to reach Sarajevo. But here he was asking her to join him, immediately, in a city at war! Just what such a move would entail was not yet clear. There would certainly be dangers, but it was right, she believed, that they should be together. It was as if the threads of her spiritual journey were coming together into a single, twisted strand, pointing the way towards Mostar: the pieces of the jigsaw were coming into place.

Born in 1966, Sandra had been raised in a traditional Catholic family in Zagreb. Prayer and religious observances had been the furniture around which her young life was built. She had been twice weekly to catechism classes, drinking in all that she was taught, hungry for a faith. Her performance at school was excellent and she left high school with top grades. She went on to study electrical engineering at university, but it was a subject for which she felt no aptitude. Her crisis point came two years into the course, when her unsuitability for it became evident and she dropped out of university, effectively unqualified.

Throughout these years, however, one area that did continue to develop was her faith. The early eagerness to learn the catechism became, in her teenage years, a search for truth and security. In common with her future husband, Nikola, whom she was still to meet, it was in a Catholic evangelistic meeting that Sandra stepped out from a family religion to a personal faith.

It had been held in a small side room in one of Zagreb's big churches, and Sandra had been struck immediately by the atmosphere of the group and its attendant sense of peace. She was filled with a longing for the deep, inner security she sensed there. Fed and nurtured by the prayers of the others, Sandra became a regular attender, and found herself changing rapidly, inheriting the very sense of inner peace she had so longed for. The group talked about an experience of being 'baptized in the Holy Spirit', an experience they saw as a doorway to a deeper intimacy with God. One evening, kneeling with other young people at the altar at the end of a prayer meeting, Sandra, too, received what she later described as the 'very, very dramatic experience' of being filled with the Holy Spirit.

A very significant change that came about through this time of prayer, of hungering after God, was the change in her ideas about fatherhood. Sandra had built up over many years a strict and authoritative picture of what a father was, and when she heard others speak of God as father, the words left her unmoved. In her own spirituality, and in her ability to trust others, she could not get past this barrier. But through the weeks and months of intimate, exhilarating prayer that the charismatic group led her into, she was able to change her picture of fatherhood, and to accept the idea of following a God called father—'Abba'. This acceptance came as a great release, and brought her a sense of personal security beyond any she had previously experienced. She was able to move on to a strong, meaningful faith around which her life, from this point on, was to be built.

Sandra was also significantly influenced at this time by Mother Teresa, whom she looked to as both model and inspiration. The Sisters of Charity had established a house in Zagreb to which many young people went as volunteers, helping to serve meals to the hungry and to keep the kitchens clean. Sandra joined this group from time to time, and was deeply influenced by the model of unselfish giving which she saw. She struggled with the prayer life she saw among the sisters, which appeared to her formal and lifeless, but she was drawn to the idea of service, of mission. She longed to find a place 'somewhere out there, somewhere where God wants me, and where the needs are greatest'. This longing was to stay with her throughout the ensuing years, and the simple image of Mother Teresa giving herself so completely to others was to be a long-lasting influence.

The next path to open up for Sandra had been unexpected, and was to take her out of Yugoslavia for the first time. Early in 1988, she had come into contact with a Swedish missionary team, working in Zagreb. The mission-aries were able to tell her of a Bible college in Sweden, The Word of Life, at which she would be able to study for a year. Sandra saw this as the ideal opportunity to test out her beliefs and refine her vision for the future, and she consequently spent the academic year of 1988–89 as a student in Sweden. She returned to Zagreb the following autumn, inspired, and clearer in her own mind about what she wanted to do with her life. But she was still burdened with difficulties at home and, even though she had now left home, she still struggled in her relationship with her father.

Through a close friend whose spiritual path was similar to her own, Sandra had previously come into contact with a Pentecostal group which was attracting many other charismatic Catholics. It was here, rather than in Catholic parish life, that she made her spiritual home on her return. She appreciated the greater freedoms of belief and worship, and the lack of liturgy and formality, although she struggled even here against legalism and ritual.

At this time, however, the very fabric of the society that Sandra had been born into and raised by was being shaken. The fall of the Berlin Wall in 1989 sent shock waves through the whole of Eastern Europe. Everyone knew that a chain reaction had started, but no one dared to guess where it might end. Throughout 1990 and well into 1991, the whole future of the Republic of Yugoslavia was in question, culminating in the 1991 referenda in Slovenia and Croatia which confirmed these regions' desire for independence, and ultimately sparking off war. In the midst of this uncertainty and change, a mounting economic crisis was bringing high levels of unemployment and hitting young people particularly hard. Sandra found temporary office jobs, but these were punctuated with periods out of work. She still had not found the place in which her longing to serve would be challenged.

It was out of such a period of turbulence and, at times, great difficulty, that Sandra came into a growing security in her relationship with Nikola. They met in May 1991 through the Zagreb Pentecostal church. After being together as members of the same crowd on one or two occasions, Nikola phoned her and asked her to meet him—just the two of them, at a cafe. They talked of a number of things, and she sensed, even then, that he was attracted to her. He chose to tell her, that first meeting, of his marriage.

Nikola had married Ana in December 1977. In 1979, their daughter Marija was born. Shortly after the birth, however, Nikola had been offered a twelve-month contract in Algiers, and by the time he returned to Zagreb, it was clear that the marriage was failing. By 1980, they were divorced. He still saw Marija often, and was a proud and committed father, but he had long since given up hope of rebuilding the marriage. When he had later become a Christian, this past failure had weighed heavily on him.

As he was telling his story, Nikola watched Sandra's every gesture. He knew full well that she could so easily reject him. Already, in the church, he was held at a distance by some, partly because of the divorce and partly because of his history as a healer. He sensed that she was nervous, perhaps afraid. Nevertheless, the rejection he had feared did not materialize, and soon afterwards, they began to go out together.

Sandra's fear, for the most part, came from knowing how her parents might react. Nikola was eleven years older than she was, divorced, and with a history considered by many to be dubious. For weeks, because of this apprehension, she fought the idea of their relationship going any deeper. Nikola, for his part, grew more and more convinced of his feelings. He was thirty-seven, and the father of a thirteen-year-old girl; yet here he was, behaving like a teenager! Every day that they didn't see each other, he would telephone Sandra, just to see how she was. And the more time they spent together, the more they enjoyed each other's company.

Over a period of weeks, Sandra began to see that she was falling in love. She told her parents about Nikola, and began to accept that theirs was an all-or-nothing relationship—that they were either meant for each other for life, or not good for each other at all. She found herself debating the question almost constantly, but moving, day by day, towards a deeper commitment.

For Sandra, it was a relationship that brought together many of the threads of her life. The more she and Nikola talked of their visions for the future, the more she saw another path opening up. She was not at all surprised the first time he proposed, though concern about her father's reaction held her back from wearing a ring. Shortly afterwards, however, in the autumn of 1992, they talked again of marriage, and this time both agreed that they should go ahead.

At this particular time, neither Sandra nor Nikola were content in the Evangelical church in Zagreb; Nikola's refugee family was no longer dependent on him. It all added up to a sense of new beginnings, which might possibly take them away from Zagreb.

Sandra and Nikola agreed to marry without knowing what this new beginning would be, but they hoped and prayed that something new would open up, even if they had to wait for it. It was only a matter of days before their answer came, in the shape of a ten-ton truck, a consignment of stoves for Mostar, and a delivery run that was to change everything.

Driving north on New Year's Eve, Nikola prepared and rehearsed, in his own mind, the four conversations which would be crucial to the decision he had to take. These were to be with Stevo, with Peter, with Milan Pavicic— an old friend in Zagreb—and, most importantly, with Sandra. If any one of these four people showed reluctance, or asked him to be cautious, he would listen. Of the four interviews, it was the last about which he was most nervous.

On the way to Zagreb, Nikola first dropped off the truck in Rijeka, and spoke to Stevo. Nikola still felt the nervousness that had previously made him hesitate. He had begun to regard Stevo as a father figure and the last thing he wanted was to let him down or appear foolish and immature before him. As he handed back the keys of the truck, he tentatively began to explain his feelings. But the rejection he had feared made no appearance. Stevo could only express gratitude that someone was willing to go to Mostar.

'It will be easier for us to find another truck-driver', he said, 'than it to find anyone willing to go to Mostar.'

Stevo had been deeply impressed by the reports he had received from Nikola during the Christmas week. He had seen a sensitivity and integrity in him, and a willingness to work, which echoed all he had guessed at and hoped for when the two had first met. Nikola's offer to help Miro confirmed the best.

'There is a Christian organization in Britain', Stevo went on to tell his friend, 'who have offered to support someone to work in these critical areas, and serve people in need. How would you feel, Nikola, if I asked them to support you?'

Nikola was dumbfounded. It was as if the first piece of some huge jigsaw was falling silently into place. So far, he was actively being encouraged in his desire to go to Mostar, when he had been expecting a set-back. Moreover, here was the possibility of an income for two years—up to this point, he had had no idea of how he and Sandra would survive financially. Just a few days earlier, he had set eyes on Mostar for the first time. Not long after that, Miro had asked if he would come and help. After two more days, he was beginning to feel that he should say 'yes'. Now, as the last hours of 1992 crept by, and with the hopes and uncertainties of a Balkan new year just around the corner, it looked as if everything might just fall into place for him to go.

From Rijeka, Nikola took the train to Zagreb. When at last they met together again, Nikola found himself almost apologizing to Sandra for the strength of his feelings about Mostar. She had already accepted so much, to make room for their relationship. How could he now ask this of her—to move to a war zone? The cease-fire had held for over a month, but who could know what the future would hold? He had been glad of her positive response when he had phoned from Mostar, but he had heard the fear in her voice. Since then, she would have had time to think and pray. If there was going to be doubt, it would be now that it would show. He knew that it had to be as strong a call for her as for him, for he could not ask her to come to Mostar on the strength of his feelings alone. They had talked so much of service, of being used in the mission of the church. Both were totally committed to this dream—it had been a part of what drew them together. But he was torn, all the same, between the opportunity to do something, to make a difference in the face of such need, and the desire to offer Sandra a happy, secure home, and a marriage of peace in a place of peace. What he really wanted was both.

'I can't make the decision for both of us', he said to Sandra, when they had talked at great length about the situation in Mostar. 'I need to know how you feel. I need to know that you are sure.'

Her response brought instant relief.

'Nothing has changed', she said. 'I still feel the way I felt when we spoke. I want to do what is right for us. If it is right for us to be in Mostar, then Mostar is where we must be.'

They still hadn't had time to buy rings, but they agreed now that it would be the first thing they did in the new year. The two decisions—to be married, and to move to Mostar—somehow confirmed one another. And Sandra's willingness to go also served, for Nikola, to strengthen the call he felt.

It was clear, however, that Sandra could not leave immediately. She was working and had obligations to see through, and there were the wedding arrangements to be made. It would have to be Nikola, in the first instance, who made the move south.

But it was not a move to be made alone. During his long journey back to Zagreb, Nikola had thought and prayed about who he might ask to come with him. There was more than enough work for two, and he knew that he would be more effective that way. Milan Pavicic had immediately come to mind as a potential partner in the work, both for the Agape programme and for the re-establishing of a church. He and Nikola had often spoken of working together, and he shared his friend's determination to *do something* in his country's time of crisis. When Nikola was therefore able to speak to Milan, the latter listened eagerly to Nikola's report, sensing in it both vision and enthusiasm. His response was immediate, and positive. He was ready to leave when asked.

Nikola's last phone call was to Peter Mackenzie, who had been anxious for news and was glad to hear his voice. It was true that they had spoken twice by telephone during Christmas week, but it was good to know that Nikola was back safely in Zagreb. Peter was interested to hear Nikola's impressions of Mostar and his experiences with the distribution of aid. But he was shocked to hear the conclusion.

'Peter,' there was a tone of gravity in Nikola's voice, 'I won't be able to drive trucks into Mostar any more.'

'I understand, Nikola,' said Peter, remembering, and forgiving, the Sarajevo refusal. 'What you've done already is enough. No one expects more of you.' He wondered if Nikola had found the trip too dangerous, too frightening, or if there had been some incident about which he had not yet been told.

'No, you don't understand,' Nikola went on, 'I believe that it is right that we should live there.'

Around the world, the year turned. Late-night news reviews on televisions across the globe showed graphic images of the year that Yugoslavia had lived through: the destruction of cities, the emaciated bodies of refugees. In perhaps a thousand different languages, commentators posed the question that every viewer anticipated: 'Will 1993 bring peace?'

Candle-lit prayers were being said at Masses in countless cities, towns and villages; millions of people set out their dreams and longings for the coming year; and tens of thousands echoed the silent words: 'Will 1993 bring peace?'

And in London and Geneva, Washington and Paris, politicians—ground down by their own powerlessness to intervene in Europe's greatest crisis in fifty years—in the last instant before letting 1992 slip by, allowed themselves one last question: 'Will 1993 bring peace?'

The same question resounded in the six troubled nations that were once Yugoslavia. It had been their most troubled year in living memory and, as 1992 drew to its agonizing end, no question mattered more. For Nikola and Sandra, caught up, like all the people of the Balkans, in circumstances they could neither control nor understand, the turning of the year held great significance. As the last few minutes of a year of tragedy and sadness drained away, they prayed and longed that 1993 would be the year of peace. Newly engaged, newly certain of their call to Mostar, they prayed that they would find a part to play in peace, and that they would play it well.

5

A Church is Born

Let it break out like blisters
On the skin of this city . . .
Let it come to us,
Let your Kingdom come.

Gerard Kelly, 'Liturgy', from *Rebel Without Applause*

MOSTAR, JANUARY 1993

A huge explosion ripped through the street, sending shock waves through the warehouse. Nikola, thrown to the floor, thought for a moment that he might be dead. Through the open door, he saw that the workers who had been standing just outside had been thrown to the ground. He was filled with panic. Crawling across the hall, he manoeuvred himself under the stairs and sat, shivering with fear. The others managed to get in from outside and join him under the flimsy protection of the stairwell, as shells continued to fall.

Nikola's hopes that the cease-fire would hold had lived for just five days. Arriving back in Mostar with Milan on 10 January, he had found the city much as he had left it, a fragile peace allowing ground for a measured optimism. But just days later, the shelling had begun again, the first shell exploding just metres from the warehouse. For a week, Nikola had lived in a constant haze of fear and shock. He had never been this close to war. He would struggle, later, to recall even one day in those first four months of 1993 on which shells did not fall. The warehouse was on the west bank of the Neretva, in a zone which was to be frequently targeted. It would not be long before it was rendered unusable: stocked with food and supplies, but too dangerous to approach.

Milan and Nikola had travelled by bus to Siroki Brijeg, which was as close to Mostar as public transport would allow. There they telephoned Miro, who came to meet them with the Croatia's Pentecostal leader, the renowned theologian, Peter Kuzmic. He had been visiting Mostar with a Swedish delegation that was later to finance staff for the Agape. They had considered it a miracle that anyone was prepared to move into Mostar at this time, and at the roadside they had gathered to pray for Nikola and Milan, before heading in two directions—the visiting delegation to Osijek, and Miro, Milan and Nikola to Mostar.

The two new arrivals had been found an apartment close to the old Agape office, and had thrown themselves into the work at the warehouse. Trucks were arriving regularly from Germany, Switzerland and Sweden, and local groups would then come to collect the food and supplies they needed. The work was physically demanding, and needed careful organization. There were already a few people who helped to unload the trucks, but few had been prepared to work hard at it. It was not long before Nikola and Milan's passionate approach was making waves, producing, in time, a transfusion of volunteers.

Nikola's conviction was that the church, which had shut down at the outbreak of war in April 1992, should be reopened as soon as possible. For him the two tasks, of distributing aid coming in from outside churches and of rebuilding a church for Mostar, could not be separated. He longed to see, at the warehouse, workers whose work was energized by a fire of faith. He believed that a living, worshipping church in the heart of the city would give renewed conviction to the work of Agape and, alongside it, could offer the spiritual and emotional consolation that was so desperately needed. Like Stevo, he had come to see that the long-term work towards forgiveness and reconciliation was as crucial as the short-term efforts of aid and relief.

Nikola had set up the first Christian meetings within days of arriving. Using Agape's former, newly vacated storage area, he and Milan would arrange an evening meeting to follow the day's work. The meetings were simple and informal, with Nikola simply sharing his own story, and his belief that the Christian faith had something to offer to Mostar. At the first such meeting, a young man, Robert Sunjic, was in tears as Nikola spoke, and had stayed afterwards to talk. He had decided then and there to become a Christian, the first, as it turned out, of many, and a member of the church to this day.

Just six or seven people had gathered for these meetings, nervously singing the Christian songs Nikola and Milan taught. For the most part they were people who had already been drawn into the work of Agape. Shortly afterwards, a woman who had been a member of the old Pentecostal church started to come, and she helped with the running of the meetings. Nikola and Milan told people of the meetings as they went about the city delivering food. The number of attenders began to grow, and a regular pattern was established. Each day, they would work in the warehouse or on deliveries; each evening they would visit those who had expressed an interest in the church; and each Sunday they would gather together for a simple service of worship and preaching.

Some of those who had come had experienced evangelicals before, and had not been impressed. At times, foreign missionaries had come, but had given the impression that they were putting on a show: it had been hard to adapt their beliefs to the culture of Mostar. Nikola and Milan took a more simple approach, without showmanship, but with an honest sharing of their beliefs. There was no room for pretension, since most of those with whom they were sharing knew them through the warehouse work. If anything they said did not hold true in daily life, it would be seen immediately. The tiny congregation grew week by week, with Miro taking over responsibility for most of the preaching, and with Nikola and Milan continuing together in the warehouse and visiting people. The Mostar church had been reborn.

Among those who came, many individuals were of mixed origin, struggling to find their identity in a fast-changing political situation. Before war broke out in Yugoslavia, at least a third of all marriages joined people of different ethnic groups. In some cities, such as Mostar, the figure was higher. Tito's vision for the Federation had included the mixing of ethnic groups, and many people had been happy to set aside former identities and think of themselves simply as Yugoslavs. A survey recently carried out by the University of Belgrade estimated that some four million people in the various republics are first-generation offspring of mixed marriages. But as power groups in each of the republics have attempted to redraw the social and political map along lines of ethnic purity, the mixed families have been at the sharp end of suffering. As Nikola, Milan and Miro kick-started the Mostar church back into life, they saw from the very start that they must offer support to such families.

One such mixed family were Jasna and Milan Vukovic, and their son, Tibor. The trials they lived through when Mostar descended into the chaos of war are a clear illustration of the pain of mixed marriage in this unique context. By the time they came to Nikola for help in January 1993, they were desperate to leave Mostar.

Jasna, a Muslim, had been born in Serbia in 1959, and came to Mostar in 1976 with her parents and her sister. Her father had been in the Yugoslav National Army. Jasna had been a free thinker, and had grown up loving rock music, art and travel; eventually she had gone on to study sculpture in Sarajevo. She also practised yoga, became a vegetarian, and hitchhiked—to London, Morocco, Germany, and Turkey (where many of her parent's relatives still live). Through a group that often climbed the mountains around Mostar seeking to get 'back to nature', she had met her future husband, Milan Vukovic, who was Serbian. In such a mixed city as Mostar, however, Jasna was determined not to take sides and she hoped, with others, to bring good vibrations into the city through meditation, pushing back the rising tide of violence.

After Jasna and Milan's son, Tibor, was born in 1991, Jasna and the baby had moved into her parents' old flat in central Mostar. Milan was working at the aluminum factory just outside town, and when the war broke out, he was unable for a few days to get back into the city.

For five months, war had torn apart the centre of Mostar. Jasna put furniture against the windows of her seventh floor apartment to protect it from shrapnel, which was known to fly up to one kilometre from an exploding shell. There was shooting in the streets, there were grenades and shells. Jasna watched Tibor take his first steps in front of the apartment block under the sound of exploding grenades. In June, Milan sent a friend with a car to take Jasna and Tibor out of the city, to the coast. They drove through the streets with grenades exploding all around, Tibor crouched down on the car floor for safety.

On the coast, Jasna found lodgings with other refugees. They lived eight to a room and huddled round a tiny radio at night to hear news of Mostar. Each day, Jasna struggled to find the food and supplies that she needed for her baby, and listened, horrified, as her fellow refugees spoke with hatred and bitterness of the Serbs, and what they deserved for all that their armies had done. At times, the hatred turned towards her, not only the wife of a Serb but the daughter of a JNA officer.

Tibor caught a fever, and he cried almost constantly. In Mostar, Jasna had taught him a game to be ready when shells fell—the long, shrill whistle making way for the 'boom'. He had grown used to war. Among the refugee families, they were away from the shelling, but his distress grew worse; he was nervous, agitated, unable to eat. Jasna was sure that Tibor needed to be in his own home. When she heard, in July, that Milan had been taken prisoner, she determined to get back to her apartment and, if possible, to trace her husband.

She had found transport back to Mostar, and had arrived to find the city relatively quiet. But in the streets, she saw the cars of a new army she had not known before: their uniforms were now emblazoned with black swastikas. She traced her husband, through the police, and was able to visit him in prison. He was taken out, each day, in work parties, building front-line installations in the mountains, or digging graves. When the party moved out across the city at 7.00 a.m. each morning, Jasna was allowed to stand with Tibor at the roadside. She tried to smile an encouragement to her husband, who otherwise walked with his eyes down. When she spoke to him, he was filled with shame for all the bitterness which now seemed to exist between the people of his culture and of hers.

In September, talks between the army chiefs brought a greater measure of peace and an exchange of prisoners. Milan was released, and offered transport to the Serbian side. Jasna begged him to stay in order that the family should be together and to try, if possible, to find refuge in another country. He moved back to the apartment, but found the political situation almost unbearable. Night after night, the television news reported, in graphic detail, crimes of one side against the other. He saw pictures of the region in which he had grown up, now destroyed. In the streets, he walked in fear that he would be killed. He had lost all contact with his own family, hearing rumours that they were dead, but with no hard facts. Just surviving from day to day became increasingly difficult. They found it hard to get food from either the Muslim or Croatian aid agencies; and they had no money. Their situation was desperate.

It was at this time that they heard that the Norwegian Government was accepting the immigration of refugees without demanding papers. Milan had cousins in Switzerland, whom he felt sure would advance them the money they needed to get to Norway. All he needed was a telephone. Jasna had heard that one of the Agape workers had a phone, and Milan knew, through a neighbour, where he lived. They arrived, with Tibor, at Nikola's door.

'We introduced ourselves to him', Jasna was later to recall. 'I said, "my husband's Serbian, I'm a Muslim, and this is our son. He's two." Nikola said, "Yes."

'When we saw his face, and he said "yes" so gently, it was the first time in two years we had met a man who has a nice face when you tell him you are in a mixed marriage.'

Telephone connection to Switzerland was impossible that night, but Nikola invited them to come back to try again.

'You have a baby', he said. 'You must need food.'

He gave them a box of supplies, but could see that they were embarrassed to receive it.

'Don't worry,' he said, 'it comes from my brothers and sisters, outside Mostar.'

Jasna and Milan were immediately drawn to Nikola. Their life had been a nightmare throughout the war, and in recent months, the only positive thing they could focus on was planning to leave. Nothing in Mostar held anything but bitterness for them. But in Nikola, they found someone positive, someone whose life was not defined by ethnic purity, selfishness or violence.

Telephones were, at this time, a rare commodity in Mostar, operating under conditions that were far from adequate. It could take hours just to get a line out of the city. When Jasna and Milan next came to use the phone, it took time to get a connection, and while they were waiting, they talked. Nikola told them how he had come to Mostar, and what the church was doing. They read the Bible together. He told them he was engaged to Sandra and was hoping that she, too, would come to Mostar soon. He had some teaching tapes in English, which he offered to Jasna for her to listen to at home.

When the call came through, Milan's cousins in Switzerland agreed to everything: they would support the whole family in the move to Norway, and would send tickets and money as soon as possible. Jasna and Milan began to believe, for the first time in two years, that things might improve for them.

They had been told that, once in Norway, it would be necessary to stay in the country for five years to establish residency; there would be no chance of visiting home during this time. Jasna had not seen her parents since they left Mostar at the onset of war, and felt that she should go to them in Serbia before leaving for Norway. She and Milan planned to travel together to Zagreb; then she would visit Serbia while he went on ahead to Norway.

They began to sell their possessions in preparation for leaving. A strange form of economics had taken over in the city at that time, with one top price for everything. Whether people were selling a washing machine or an apartment, they could not expect more than 200–300 German Marks, the only currency accepted by everyone in the city. Jasna sold a washing machine for 200 marks and a car, for which she had paid 2,000, for 150 marks. They gave away other things, and organized the documents with which they would need to leave.

Even as the preparations gathered speed, Jasna was uneasy. Milan was desperate to leave, fearing for his life each day he remained in Mostar, and for Tibor, it was better to be out of the city. Their situation was terrifying. Jasna listened to the tapes Nikola had given her, and sat up late into the night thinking, over and over, about all they had been through.

She looked at Tibor, asleep on the bed. In her youth, she had read Saint-Exupery's *The Little Prince*, and had longed for such a friend with whom to share her life. Now here was Tibor, her little prince, lying on a bed, in Mostar, in a war, with no safe haven. She was chain-smoking, trembling, crying.

'I was on my knees', she later recalled. 'I didn't know what to do. The best relief I'd had was painting, sculpture. But now I felt in my heart that all that I had in my life, everything, was being destroyed. I remembered my former philosophy, my travelling, my studies, all the sculptures I'd left broken in Sarajevo, all the pictures I'd painted now under the ruins of a cafe in Mostar. And I saw that there was no philosophy, no sculpture, no painting—no happiness in my life. I felt in pain. And in that moment, something happened in my heart. It was like it is when you are crying, and someone comes to you, to hold you. I felt someone come and take everything, holding me in their arms.

'I knew I was alone in the room, and I knew, inside, that this was God. The words from the tape I had listened to were still in my mind, and one word, one name, came to me: Jesus. I felt love, and I started to pray.'

It was to be several more weeks before Jasna found her way into the church, but her life was utterly changed by this occasion and, months later, when Milan had gone on ahead to Norway, Nikola and Sandra were to become her closest friends. For Nikola, Jasna's decision to become a Christian was a stepping stone in the building of the church. In common with many of those who joined the church at this stage, her decision was made alone, and in private. There were no big meetings, with drawn out appeals and orchestrated responses. There were no massed choirs. The little church simply gathered around one audacious idea: that in a city from which all hope had been drained, new life was possible.

Nikola, Miro and Milan Pavicic continued the weekly pattern of work, and each Sunday saw new people, like Jasna and Milan, drawn into their gatherings. Some were Christians already, and found encouragement in the meetings. Many were not, and came through curiosity, sitting on the sidelines for several weeks before deciding to become part of the group. By February, there were about ten or twelve people who met each Sunday, and the work of Agape was growing more effective by the day.

In Mostar, the Bosnian and Croat armies were working together against the Serbs, but with separate headquarters and command structures. There was growing tension between them, matching the divisions in the wider population. When the Serbs were driven out of the city, many Muslims came in, often driven in turn from their homes in the surrounding villages. Their arrival swelled the Muslim population of the city, already the majority.

It was clear, even then, that pushing the Serbs out of Mostar was not the end of the story. The city was tense, dark and frightening. From outside, the shelling of the JNA posed a continuing threat, with children and young people the most frequent victims. But on the inside, too, there was the dark, rising threat of further war: war that had seemed almost unthinkable a few months earlier.

On Mostar's outskirts, the mass graves of Croats and Muslims killed during the Serbian withdrawal had been uncovered: here were the corpses of hundreds of men, women and children shot at point-blank range with automatic weapons.

Access to and from the city was tightly controlled. Each of the power groups was determined to keep its own population high, in order not to lose even a metre of territory by default. Every road in or out of Mostar was blocked by numerous checkpoints manned—often, by different militias. The train station was deserted and derelict—the last train had left for Zagreb, on 8 April 1992. In the isolated city, there was a terrible, deepening sense of 'digging in', a sense that the worst was yet to come.

The Vance–Owen partition plan, the final result of the Geneva talks, had been rejected at the beginning of January 1993. The plan, calling for ten autonomous provinces within Bosnia-Hercegovina, was intended to keep the newest nation in Europe intact. But all three parties to the talks rejected it. In principle they agreed to a cease-fire; but in reality, the three pieces of paper produced by the talks—the cease-fire proposal, a political agreement and the 'Ten Provinces' map—all remained unsigned. Some of the best political minds in the world were contributing to the peace effort and everyone had something to say, but nothing could cut into the war on the ground. The hopes that the new year would bring a new peace were quickly running dry.

Still in Zagreb at this time, Sandra had the difficult task of hearing news from Mostar but being too far removed to be involved in any way. She talked with Nikola almost daily by telephone, helping him particularly over the shock of the first days of shelling. She was living alone, and had to use a friend's telephone, which Nikola would call at a prearranged time each day. If the shelling was bad, he would sit under a table to telephone her. She, for her part, would sit on the floor in her friend's hallway. At times, Nikola would be exhausted and discouraged and Sandra would read to him over the phone from Christian books and articles. But more often, he told her excitedly of the birth of the church, of meeting Jasna and the others. He was anxious for her to join him.

'I'm sorry, Miss Baljkas, but you will not be able to be married unless you have the right papers.'

The official spoke as kindly as could be expected, but was implacable. Sandra had been unable to bring all of Nikola's papers, since everything relating to his former marriage and divorce had been left behind in Novi Varos, now under Serb occupation.

'What can we do?' she asked. 'He is in Mostar, and we need to set a date.'

'If you can get the papers to me, you can set a date one month ahead. If not, I don't know what to suggest. You will have to ask Mr Skrinjaric to come back to Zagreb for an interview.'

Sandra left the office discouraged and confused. She had not thought, when Nikola left for Mostar, that it would be so difficult to arrange the wedding.

She did manage to find a friend from Novi Varos who was able to trace some of the papers. But it was not enough; there were still some certificates missing—they were either destroyed or buried under some pile of rubble in the heart of Krajina. Even in wartime, it seemed, you still needed every piece of paper, with the right rubber stamp. She waited anxiously for Nikola's next call.

'I have to come back to Zagreb, next week', he told her, before she had even had time to tell him the problems. 'There is a truck to be collected from Germany, for Agape. I'll come first to Zagreb.'

'You'll need to', said Sandra. She went on to explain the situation with the authorities, and how important it was for Nikola to get to Zagreb as soon as possible. The truth was, it was also important for them to have some time together.

As soon as they met again in Zagreb, they both realized that they were utterly exhausted. Nikola had been working every waking hour, under intense pressure, for the first time in his life under the sound of shelling. Sandra, too, had been under pressure, both from a severe viral infection earlier in the month and from the obstacles to their marriage. They decided that they would both go to Germany, to get a couple of days of rest and peace together. In the event, the truck was not ready for them, and they had to wait a few days, staying with relatives of Nikola's. This proved to be a time of refreshment for them both. As later events would prove, it was a time they very much needed.

By mid-February, Nikola had been able, in Zagreb, to settle the problems regarding the civil wedding, and the date was set for exactly one month later: 13 March. This done, they had to decide where to hold the church wedding, which would take place the following Sunday. Sandra was happy to be married anywhere. In the end, it was Nikola who made the choice. He wanted to be married in a place that could genuinely be called their church, a place in which they could come to feel at home, and among friends. They would be married in Mostar.

6

Two Weddings and a
Lesson in War

Ahead of us, the sky's a geyser now.
A calm voice talks of cloud, yet we feel lost.
Air pockets jolt our fears and down we go.
Travellers, at this point, can only trust.

Seamus Heaney, 'Honeymoon Flight'

MOSTAR, MARCH 1993

Nikola returned to Mostar to deliver the truck from Germany, but was back in Zagreb by 13 March. The civil wedding went well, and was a joyful occasion. For both Nikola and Sandra, it was the end of a long and complex road. They left immediately for Mostar.

Peter Mackenzie had agreed to come to Mostar to perform the church wedding. They had been witnesses at the civil ceremony, and Peter was the only ordained minister, at that time, in contact with the Mostar church. As a newborn church, still tiny, the group in Mostar had no traditions or rules for weddings. Most of the members had been churchgoers for less than a year and everything they did was for the first time. Peter had previously translated most of the Methodist Service Book into Croatian, and was able to use it for the wedding ceremony.

Sandra had never been to Mostar before. She and Nikola had arrived late in the afternoon on a clouded, grey day, to the sound of shelling: it seemed oppressive, and dark. But the next morning was sunny and bright; it was a fine spring day, and Nikola was able to show his new bride around the city. Gladly taking on the role of a tour guide, he showed her the warehouse and many of the places he had come to know, including, of course, the Stari Most.

The bridge, which was then still standing, was covered by a makeshift roof of corrugated iron—scant protection against the shells. Already it was damaged; the towers at each end and, in places, the bridge itself had taken several hits.

'The men who built this roof', Nikola told Sandra, 'risked their lives to do so. Some have been killed trying to protect this bridge.'

They walked through the old city, where the Stara Carsija (the old bazaar) remains the hub of Ottoman Mostar. Here, Sandra saw for the first time how severe the shelling of east Mostar had been. She could imagine how this area must have been in peacetime: the narrow streets, the craftsmen selling their works, shops spilling out their wares onto the street, people, noise, colours and smells. Now it was quiet, grey, tense. The few people there were just stood or sat around. Sandra had never before come into the heart of an Eastern city; she sensed the difference immediately and felt conspicuous as a pale northerner in what had already become a Muslim enclave. Even in March 1993, when the Croat–Muslim alliance was, in theory, still in force in Mostar, crossing from west to east was to cross between two worlds that were tangibly different—so much had already been done to separate the two cultures. Sandra was shocked by the extent of the difference, by the intensity she felt in walking through the old town.

From the members of the church, there was a huge welcome for Sandra. Nikola had talked incessantly about her, anticipating almost daily this moment of her arrival, and the young community received her with open arms.

The old warehouse, now regularly in use as a church, had been further transformed for the wedding, and was decorated with flowers. A stonemason who was in touch with the church had donated a huge marble cross, which was delivered the day before the wedding, though not to universal acclaim.

'We are a war church', some said. 'We shouldn't have such luxuries.'

'This is not a graveyard', said others.

The cross was, of course, for the church itself as much as for the wedding, but the incident provided a remarkable window into the lives of these new churchgoers, who were not used to religious symbols. These were people for whom Christianity was not about temples and marble, but about community and peace.

The wedding itself was simple: there were no bridesmaids, no speeches. Walking to the church in her white dress with flowers in her hair, Sandra heard someone call out, 'Look, there's a bride!' She wondered how many people in Mostar had not seen a wedding since the war began.

About fifty people crowded into the tiny church for the ceremony. Less than half of these were regular church members, and others had been drawn in to witness the event. Many of them were intrigued that anyone who had a choice should want to marry in Mostar. So many people had left the city when war broke out. It was unusual, if not unique, to find new arrivals.

The service was informal. Peter had brought a guitar, and led the congregation with a few songs. He gave Sandra and Nikola each a sheet with their vows printed out. He spoke briefly about the marriage relationship, as a model of each person's relationship with God; he explained how they had a choice, to reject or respond to the love God offered them. For many people, the vows they witnessed Sandra and Nikola make to each other were an echo of the vows they themselves were making in their faith: vows to accept the love of God, to be committed to this new church, and to work, with this young couple, towards reconciliation and peace.

After the ceremony, a makeshift *svadba* (wedding feast) had been set up in the small room available in the church building. Home-made food and cakes had been provided, and the wedding guests crowded in, to eat standing up. The day provided a stark contrast to traditional Bosnian weddings, in which, under normal circumstances, great ceremonies are followed by lavish feasts: family, friends and neighbours are invited into the celebrations in large numbers, and there are speeches, music, enormous quantities of food, and many presents. Sandra and Nikola had none of this. But they found their day, nonetheless, memorable and deeply moving. This was the first wedding the church had enjoyed, and in a sense, it marked the church's coming of age. What began with six or seven aid workers gathering in an old warehouse was now, legitimately, a church. It would prove to be a significant day in the lives of many, not just of the bride and groom.

Among the guests were Jasna and Milan Vukovic. Jasna had warmed to Sandra immediately, and was deeply moved to be at the wedding: she felt it a privilege to be invited. She had challenged Milan, saying that together, in the church, they should start a new life built not on fighting and competition but on the peace that was here among this group of believers. She saw in Sandra and Nikola two friends who could make such a hope into a reality. The speed at which she grew to love and trust them illustrates the intensity brought, by war, to relationships. This was a key feature of the early months of the Mostar church: relationships developed and matured over the space of days which in peacetime might have taken weeks, or even years, to grow.

'Before I met you', Jasna said to the bride and groom, 'I had no hope in this city. Everything here was bad for me. When I look at you, your happiness together, I have hope: I can believe that there is something good in Mostar.'

When Sandra explained that they would be travelling north straight after the wedding to stay in the mountains near Konjic, Jasna was devastated. The papers for the move to Norway could come through any day, and she knew she would probably be gone by the time her new friends returned. She hugged Sandra, weeping all the time. Neither thought they would ever see the other again.

71

The couple's trip north had been arranged as a kind of half-honeymoon. Miro was in touch with his wife's relatives in the mountainous region around Konjic who were interested in extending the work of Agape into their area. They were stonemasons, the same ones who had provided the controversial marble cross. It was agreed that Sandra and Nikola would visit them, spending a week together in the mountains and at the same time assessing the possibilities for Agape. This decision was wrong, Sandra angrily told Nikola later. She had barely had time to get used to Mostar. She had hoped to stay there, and to get to know the people of the church better. As things turned out she was right for more reasons than she could have known at the time. They travelled north, not to a week of peace and quiet, but to a honeymoon under siege.

The town of Jablanica, and the lake of the same name, are high in the mountains on the Mostar road to Sarajevo, west of Konjic and south of Prozor. The region had been largely spared during the first war, because Muslim and Croat neighbours had banded together to form a defence force. But civil death and displacement had produced ominous cracks in the alliance, and there had been tension throughout the winter of 1992. But in March 1993, Mostar was not yet implicated.

When Sandra and Nikola travelled north to a borrowed house in the mountains above Jablanica, they had no idea that the tensions and flashpoints of the winter were about to erupt into all-out war. At the Muslim checkpoint coming out of the city, the Mostar licence plates were removed from their car, an ominous warning of the tensions in the area into which they were headed. Old Yugoslavian licence plates, still in use in Bosnia, always had the red communist star between the letters and the numbers. In Croatia, and in Croat-held territories of Bosnia, this had been replaced by the chequered shield. This tiny symbol, barely visible under the dust and mud, could be the difference between driving in peace and being used as a mortar target, or worse.

Even as they were driving, they realized that in this previously Croatian area, many of the incoming Muslim refugees were now openly fighting against the Croats. Nikola and Sandra's host, the stonemason, led them to his family home, an isolated mountainside farm where three families were now living in siege conditions.

For a week Nikola and Sandra shared their honeymoon with these three families. Daily, the fathers and sons of the families would go out with rifles to the borders of the farm, while the women and children remained inside. No one knew at what moment the Bosnian forces would come. It was impossible to travel, unsafe to leave. For the first time, Nikola and Sandra tasted the Croat–Muslim war. They couldn't help but wonder what these developments might mean for Mostar.

The crisis brought into focus, for Nikola, the issue of pacifism. In Zagreb, he had refused to take a rifle, saying that, if he was called into the army, he would do some other work. Once he had become involved in humanitarian projects, he was not called up. His stance had been that it was not the army, but the killing, that he could not accept. The situation in Jablanica was different. This was not a question of being drafted. This was one household: the women and children inside, the men outside with rifles. Further away, in the hills and on the roads around, there were sounds and rumours of war. It was no longer a question of deciding, in principle, whether to fight, but of knowing, in practice, what to do if hostile forces came.

Nikola decided to accept the rifle offered to him, even though it was old, dating back to the Second World War, and he had no idea how to use it. He took his place with the other men of the tiny, besieged community, but was able to persuade them all that they would only use their weapons in defence: they would not shoot first. The experience helped Nikola to understand more fully the implications of war—how easily people can be drawn into it, how hard it is to stand totally against the use of guns when, by so doing, the lives of women and children are endangered. In those few days, he went through a crash-course in the dynamic between war and peace, a course experienced by hundreds of thousands of people in the communities of Croatia and Bosnia. As well as the violent, the enraged and the war-mongers, the Balkans have seen, these last few years, a great wave of reluctant soldiers: people who would not fight if it were not their own homes and families that were threatened. If history teaches anything about such matters, it is that war is never simple.

In time, the besieged families received news of a local cease-fire, and thought it would soon be safe to travel. Nikola and Sandra, together with a woman who wanted to get out of the area with her young son, returned to Mostar.

Once back in the city, however, they found they had to leave straight away, this time to drive across Europe to England. Stevo had, by this time, confirmed that Nikola and Sandra would be the ones to receive financial support from the United Kingdom, raised through the youth programme at Spring Harvest. He had arranged for Nikola and Sandra, with Peter Mackenzie and Boris Kacarevic, to visit the conference.

UNITED KINGDOM, SPRING 1993

In all, Nikola and Sandra spent three weeks in the United Kingdom, visiting conference sites at Ayr, Skegness, Minehead and Pwllheli. At each site, they simply told the story of the infant Mostar church, and of their own back-grounds, the decision to marry, and their to move to the city. The response was overwhelming. The thousands of British Christians gathered for the event took Sandra and Nikola to heart, warming to their faith and courage. Teenagers, in particular, were moved by what they heard, and went on to raise funds that would keep the couple for two years.

Sandra and Nikola met, amongst others, the entertainer, Roy Castle, who was fighting his own war against cancer and from which he died just eighteen months later. He was deeply impressed by the courage he saw in these two young leaders, which mirrored, somehow, the courage he had seen in many cancer patients. He, too, had been greatly encouraged by the support and prayers expressed by guests at Spring Harvest, and he spoke of Sandra and Nikola with great warmth:

With scarce resources they have brought life and faith into the hearts of many young people in Mostar. I'm proud to support the Spring Harvest Youth Appeal in helping the teenagers of Britain to raise money to bring hope to lives of teenagers in Bosnia.

Just as thousands at Spring Harvest had signed a card a year earlier to wish Roy well in his struggles, so now they signed cards and messages for the people of Mostar. In the children's meetings, a roll of wallpaper was used to record greetings from the children of Britain to the children of Mostar. The roll still hangs on the wall of the Mostar church.

At Spring Harvest, faced with the daunting task of speaking to crowds of thousands, Sandra and Nikola displayed a new courage and conviction. Speaking of things which were desperately important to them, of the nightmare their country was living through, of the fear and darkness that had come into so many people's hearts, they found that they could speak with passion and certainty, and without fear. Just as the growth of relationships in the church seemed to be accelerated by crisis, so Sandra and Nikola's personal growth was accelerated by the tasks they found themselves engaged in. By the time they left Spring Harvest, they had both come of age as Christian leaders.

After three weeks attending conferences, they were able to enjoy the elusive honeymoon. A Christian group offered them free accommodation in south-east England, and they were able, at last, to spend time in private, away from the pressures either of war or of endless interviews. They were both exhausted, and were glad of the time of rest. It was a time of refreshment that the coming months would prove more than necessary.

The church in Mostar continued to meet, in the absence of its young leaders. A team visiting from the United States held some additional meetings, one of which led to a new and significant addition to the church: the family of Janos and Razija Hudec. Janos, Hungarian by descent, was a well-known accountant in Mostar who worked with many of the large local businesses. In the final years of Communism, he had become Party president of one of the districts of the city. He was also a member of the management committee of the Mostar Judo Club, a role which was later to prove vital. Razija was Muslim and the home that she and her husband shared was right in the centre of Mostar, on what was soon to become the front line. Janos had already met Nikola, through contacts with Agape, and had been at the wedding, but it was while Sandra and Nikola were away that he and the entire Hudec family converted to Christianity.

The outbreak of war had left the Hudec family out of work and penniless. Janos had previously done well through local businesses, but local businesses had ceased to exist from the beginning of the first war. Most of the heavy industry in Mostar was spread out along the eastern valley towards Nevesinje. Most of the factory buildings still stood, but inside they had been sacked and looted; not a single machine worked. Occasionally, businesses had folded when their owners, who had more money than most with which to escape, left the area. Administrators like Janos had been left with nothing to administer, and therefore had no income. Even people who had carried on working, in the electricity or telephone services, for instance, had done so without pay.

Months later, Nikola had seen what this meant at first hand, when Janos had asked to borrow a few dinars, the equivalent of a few pennies, to pay for a certificate being issued by his daughter's school. Both men had been in tears as the few coins changed hands.

Janos and Razija had applied for emigration to Australia, and were waiting for papers. They had heard so much about ethnic 'cleansing' and persecution, even before the second war broke out in Mostar, that they held little hope, as a mixed family, of finding a permanent peace in Bosnia. Like millions, they were in danger of rejection by all sides, and didn't know where to turn. They took immediately to the little Christian community of the Mostar church, and soon became a key family in the church. Many who were later to join the community did so as a result of the influence of Janos and Razija.

Some time later, Janos arrived unannounced at Nikola's house in the company of five men. Every one of them was a manager from one of Mostar's businesses: men who had known Janos as a successful accountant and a Communist. He had brought them so that Nikola could tell them more about the Christian faith and what it would mean to be a Christian in the Mostar of the 1990s. The wider Hudec family, too, were drawn into the church. Razija's relatives, all Muslims, were all opposed to her conversion at first; but in time they changed their views, so much so that her sister, at first the strongest opponent, was later to join the church.

Even while at Spring Harvest, Nikola and Sandra heard about these new additions to the Mostar church: it seemed to be growing spontaneously, as if it had been enough simply to leave the door open. They were anxious to return, anxious to renew contact with their new-found friends, and anxious to see the church stabilize and grow further. But they didn't know, and couldn't know from the safe distance of Britain, how difficult their re-entry into Mostar would be. How could they know in advance about the tragic, bloody circumstances of 9 May 1993?

It was during the early months of 1993 that the Bosnian war had hit new depths of inhumanity and terror, making the first war, the grab for land, seem almost innocent. International commentators had feared, from as early as 1990, the implications of a breakup of Bosnia. For most of 1992, they had seen Serbia as the aggressor. But it was in 1993 that the inter-ethnic tensions of Bosnia began to outdo the previous atrocities for ferociousness and horror, and that guilt began to be apportioned more widely across the three groups. From the very start of the Yugoslav crisis, there had been the release of a chaotic, uncontrollable anger. But it reached its most chaotic, its least controllable, in the fighting in Bosnia in 1993.

Alongside the hastily formed national armies, there sprung up local militias, maverick gangs, and criminal groups masquerading as political fighters. Names like 'The Condors' and 'The Black Knights' began to appear on graffiti to join the already common paintings of national emblems. In some cases, inter-group rivalry led to death and injury as surely as inter-ethnic war. The longer it took the politicians to come up with a Bosnian solution, the more vicious the fighting by all the different factions became. It was as if political impotence proved that genocide was the only workable plan. And for every act of violence and hatred, there was the potential for an even worse act of revenge—a principle of multiplication which, more than any other factor, has been responsible for violence spreading like a forest fire through Bosnia. And revenge will probably be the greatest of all barriers to lasting peace.

Where other regions in Europe found new cause for hope in 1993, it seemed that Bosnia was destined to slip deeper into despair.

Even twenty-four hours before the Owen–Vance partition plan was rejected, President George Bush had declared, 'Today, the Cold War is over', and Boris Yeltsin had declared the Start-2 Treaty, signed by the two men in Moscow on 3 January. It was hailed as 'a major step towards fulfilling the centuries-old dream of disarmament'. Peace began in one part of Europe. But war tightened its grip in another. And Mostar began to crack under the strain of its old nightmare of disunity.

Bush's successor, Bill Clinton, was inaugurated just a few weeks later, on 20 January, in Washington DC. The group Fleetwood Mac were re-formed for the event, and sang 'Don't Stop Thinking About Tomorrow'. But Clinton was to find before long that it was Bosnia he couldn't stop thinking about, as US foreign policy became more and more influential in the crisis. Diplomats who thought that they could offer advice on the situation from the outside found that this was complex: their every word, threat, sanction or failure had a part to play. Even aid convoys under the supervision of the United Nations became part of the war, as roadblocks, hijacks and looting cynically withheld supplies from those who most needed them and seemed to spit in the face of every international diplomatic effort.

Two months later, *Time Magazine* declared that even food had become 'a new weapon in Bosnia', as food supplies to the 380,000 residents of Sarajevo were stopped. This enforced hunger strike was a protest at the blockades of food supplies by the Serbs to Muslim enclaves in eastern Bosnia. Just days later, *Time Magazine* published the tallies of death and destruction in Bosnia since May 1992: 20,000 raped; 70,000 detention camp inmates; 130,000 killed; 740,000 refugees still within Bosnia; and over 1,000,000 refugees elsewhere. Other sources doubled some of these figures, confirming that they represented a conservative estimate. An earlier report by European Community investigators had confirmed that in Bosnia, 'rape is not an incidental of war but a weapon of war to force people to leave their homes'.

In Britain, two ten-year-old boys were charged, in February 1993, with the murder of the toddler, James Bulger. The public reaction was enormous, sparking debate throughout Britain on the raising of children in a violent society. One month later, just as Nikola Skrinjaric was showing his new bride around Mostar for the first time, an IRA bomb ripped through Warrington town centre, busy with Mother's Day shoppers, killing Jonathan Bell, aged three, and Tim Parry, aged twelve. The public outcry sparked a demonstration by 10,000 in Dublin one week later. The massive expression of emotion at the horror of the deaths of three children puts in context the horror of Bosnia, where the deaths are counted in thousands, and quantity somehow sanitizes atrocity. The names of Jamie Bulger, Jonathan Bell and Tim Parry were known, quite rightly, in almost every home in Britain. The names of the dead children of Bosnia are remembered, for the most part, only by their families.

The Vance–Owen plan, was signed on behalf of the Muslim Bosnian Government at the UN Headquarters in New York on 25 March. Just one month later, the Bosnian Serbs overwhelmingly rejected the same plan, despite the threat of harsh new economic sanctions against Serbia itself. Like an enormous and frightening rollercoaster ride, the prospects for peace rose and fell. Unlike a rollercoaster ride, however, there was no guarantee of a happy ending, and there were no safety straps, no end in sight. Each time hopes rose, they stayed up for a shorter time. Each time they fell, they fell deeper. And all the time the tally of death, the scourge of ethnic 'cleansing', and the stockpiling of potential for revenge went on.

In Mostar, the Serb shelling of the city centre continued, the old city of the east now all but rubble. The gradual separation of Croats and Muslims to west and east went on, gathering pace, losing inhibition. The strategic importance of Mostar increased with every failure of international talks. For the Muslim government, Mostar was a crucial staging-post on the route from Sarajevo to the sea: without it, they were unlikely to survive. For the Croats, Mostar was the potential capital of the self-proclaimed republic of Bosnia-Hercegovina, currently run from the small town of Grude.

For the people of Mostar, already bruised and shell-shocked from twelve months of fighting with the Serbs, the prospect of escalating conflict was terrifying. The last

Stevo Dereta with Gerard Kelly (left) and Lowell Sheppard (right) outside the Pizzeria Dionis, Rijeka, Croatia
(LARRY RUSSELL)

Stevo Dereta, whose plea for a driver to take vital aid into war-stricken Mostar started this remarkable story
(JIM LORING)

Some of the refugees at Camp Hidroelektra, Ucka near Rijeka
(JIM LORING)

Janos Hudec and family with Sandra Skrinjaric (right)
(BEECH/SEATON)

Children on the coach returning to Mostar from Crikvenica in September 1993
(BEECH/SEATON)

Sandra and Nikola Skrinjaric
(BEECH/SEATON)

View from Janos's appartment across the fromt line to the city centre in September 1993
(BEECH/SEATON)

Sandra and Nikola with Emilija (second from left) and friends
(BEECH/SEATON)

Nikola on the temporary bridge that replaces the 16th-century Stari Most, destroyed in the fighting in November 1993
(LOWELL SHEPPARD)

Jasmina in September 1994
(LOWELL SHEPPARD)

Tibor and his mother Jasna
(LOWELL SHEPPARD)

Dedication ceremony for Sandra and Nikola's baby daughter Viktorija, September 1994 (LARRY RUSSELL)

A recent bullet hole in the church door is witness to the continuing violence in September 1994
(LARRY RUSSELL)

Anita and Drazen, the second couple to be married in the church since war broke out

(LOWELL SHEPPARD)

The late Roy Castle offered his support for Sandra and Nikola's work when they met him on a visit to Britain in January 1994

(TERRY WALKER)

A children's playground amid the rubble of east Mostar

(LOWELL SHEPPARD)

get worse. Journalist Ed Vulliamy later wrote this despairing statement in his commentary on the Bosnian war, *Seasons in Hell*:

On the ground, Bosnia's war is where the worst always happens. You hope something cannot be true, but you fear it might be, and it is. You hope that the next stage in the grotesque and tragic logic of the war will be averted, but you hope in vain.

Hope, a rare and valuable commodity at the best of times, was in desperately short supply in the Mostar of May, 1993.

7
Balkan Beirut

*If everyone were to follow the eye-for-an-eye
principle of justice, the whole world would go
blind.*

Mahatma Gandhi

MOSTAR, MAY 1993

In his moving account of four years as a hostage in Beirut, *An
Evil Cradling*, Brian Keenan recounts a visit made before his
kidnap to a cinema in the city. The film, he remembers, was a
war story set in Vietnam, strong on action, weak on analysis:
an orgy of violence and death. What he was struck by,
however, did not happen on screen, but off it. He recalls:

*We sat there in the darkened cinema, and as each character
pulled out his weapon and began firing furiously, the young
Arab men around us would groan and moan in a kind of ecstasy,
crying out the names of the weapons. All around us we could
hear the words 'Kalashnikov, Kalashnikov; Beretta, Beretta.'
These young men knew the names of every type of gun, even the
names of mortars and rocket-launchers. The cinema rang with a
chant of excited worship.'*

Gun fever is a strange disease that takes over at a time when
all else has failed, when violence has run amok so long that the
rules of decency by which such actions might be expected to be
restrained have been erased. Men and women have heard for
long enough that their enemies have raped their wives and
sisters; they have, too often, buried their children in
unmarked, mass graves. Given the chance, they will drive
these enemies from their homes. But by so doing, they will
also wipe out every human value they have held sacred.

Keenan's further description of the young people of Beirut holds some of the visible symptoms of this fever:

He carries his Kalashnikov on his arm, his handgun stuck in the waistband of his trousers, a belt of bullets slung around his shoulders ... The guns were symbols of potency. The men were dressed as caricatures of Rambo.

The description of Beirut in 1985 has disturbing parallels in the Mostar of less than ten years later, when this same gun fever gripped the city. Ed Vulliamy, writing in 1993, named Mostar 'the real Beirut of the Balkans'.

Like every war, Mostar's battles were about power and territory, about frontiers drawn on a map, about fear, anger, and revenge. But there was something deeper still at work in Bosnia, a level of hatred beyond the realms of rational behaviour.

For 400 years, Mostar had been the gateway between the West and the East, between Christianity and Islam. Under Tito, the forced subjection of both these faiths to the greater socialist ideal brought a measure of integration. In the best of worlds, it was called pluralism, even if, in the worst, it was also called oppression. Either way, there remained a significant fault line beneath the surface, a deeply distinct difference between two cultures.

Of all the derelict sites in Mostar after two years of bombardment, one of the most disturbing was the site of the mosque at the very heart of the west side—not because of the mess it was left in, but precisely the opposite. There were other buildings which stood as battered skeletons testifying to the ferocity of war, but this site had something else to say. Here there were no broken beams, no piles of rubble. Instead, every stone, every speck of dust that had been part of the mosque had been cleared away, leaving a patch of gravel and weeds about the size of a small shoppers' car park. Nothing was left to show that this was once a place of worship. The building had not so much been destroyed as obliterated, erased from the landscape with utter precision, as if it had never existed. A similar fate was suffered by one of the Orthodox churches in east Mostar.

It was this clinical determination to destroy, to rid the very soil of every sign of another's faith, that it is now hardest to fit into any strategic picture of the Bosnian war. But without it, the war cannot be understood. What began as a fight over territorial control became a fight between cultures: for extremists on all sides, it became no less than a fight to the death and every atrocity must be reinterpreted in the light of this ethnic strife.

Without acknowledging this fever—this disease that ate away at human reason until only raw anger remained—it would be impossible to account for the history of Mostar since 9 May 1993. On that day, a Sunday, the tension that had been building in the city for months, and which had already wreaked havoc in the surrounding mountain areas, erupted into violence and bloodshed. The second war broke out in Mostar.

Emilija Jupek, a teenager who was later to join the church, was sixteen at the time. She remembers the fighting beginning at 5.00 a.m.

'There was terrible shooting, fire, screaming, people running in the streets. I didn't know what was happening. I jumped off my bed to look out of the window, and my father said "lie down, it could be that they will send bombs."

'I didn't leave the apartment for ten days. During that time they came to the building and asked if there were any Muslims there, to take them to the other side. All the time there was terrible fighting. I didn't know what they were doing: first with the Serbs and now this with the Muslims. I had already lost all my Serb friends: I didn't want to lose my Muslim friends too.'

During the ten days, Emilija's father was able to bring in supplies of macaroni, dried milk, and bread. The fighting moved around the city: no front line had been established at this stage. Each day, a different building would be the focus of the shooting. Each day the division of the city into a Croatian, Catholic west and a Bosnian, Muslim east became more pronounced.

Each day, a new sector would be 'ethnically cleansed'. Andelko Matinovic, director of the Mostar Children's Home, was in his apartment in old Mostar on the morning of 9 May. Within minutes of the fighting breaking out, an armed unit of the Bosnian army came to take from him the keys to the Children's Home, for which they had some purpose in mind. The home, destroyed in the first war, had been rebuilt in late 1992, with money from a Swiss relief agency and, just the day before, eighty refugees had been placed there. Andelko never found out what happened to them after 9 May. He and his wife were was taken to the prison in east Mostar, where they were kept for twenty days. Their release, on 21 May, had been negotiated with UN help, but when they came out of prison, they found their apartment destroyed and burnt out, their car a charred wreck, and all their belongings looted. Andelko's mother, who had lived in west Mostar, had died while he was in custody. She had been ill for some time, and Andelko took many months to come to terms with the fact that he was not with her when she died.

Andelko found out that one of the commanders of a Muslim sniper unit, covering a section of the now stabilized front line, was a friend. He begged him to allow him to cross the ten metres of no man's land to attend his mother's funeral. Urgent radio messages had been passed by his relatives asking him to come. But they would not allow him: there was to be no crossing of the line—the least movement in the ten-metre stretch would draw fire, probably from both sides.

When UN intervention won Andelko and his wife permission, on 29 May, to cross the line, they did so with one suitcase which contained everything that they now owned. They walked away from the Muslim snipers, sheltering at one end of the street, until, halfway down, a voice shouted that they should stop. Croatian soldiers emerged from hiding to take them, at gunpoint, to the side of the road. They were held, arms against the wall, and searched. They had no papers.

At this moment, Andelko and his wife were seen by two snipers, high in the new bank building that towered above the front line positions.

'Are you going to shoot them, or shall I?' said one, nonchalantly.

'Let's just wait and see who they are', said the other.

'Let's do it now', the first insisted.

'No, wait', his comrade said, and in that moment recognized his friend Andelko.

Esad and Zvjezdana Dedic—she a Croatian Catholic, he a Muslim working in the Croat military police—were apart when the fighting broke out. Esad had been called out the night before to a problem outside the city, leaving Zvjezdana and her baby, Jasmina, alone in their apartment. Jasmina was then just four days past her first birthday. Esad arrived back after the conflict had begun. The family were relatively safe during those first few days. Once reunited, they worked, slowly but surely, to put concrete blocks in all their windows. It would be sixteen months before they were removed, and even then the blocks stayed in the hall, just in case.

Janos and Razija lived in the same block, 200 metres from the Neretva valley, in an area fast becoming the front line. They did not brick their windows. Weeks later, they would dig out, from the plaster of their dining room wall, the bullets from a sniper's gun. Within days of the 9 May, they would be one of only eight families left in a block that had had forty-six apartments. They had nowhere else to go. They would spend much of 1993 in the basement.

Jasna, on 9 May, was in her apartment with her son, Tibor. She heard shelling and explosions in the distance from 5.00 a.m., and listened as it went on, hour after hour. She knew that it meant that Muslims and Croats were now fighting each other. From her window she saw that the streets were deserted except for the soldiers who would occasionally appear at the side of a building. She thought immediately of her sister, living a few blocks away and married to a Muslim, who had refused to take up arms and was caught now, on the 'wrong' side of town. The couple's youngest child had been born just months before, in January. At 9.00 a.m., Jasna heard a sharp, insistent knocking at her door, and she opened it to face a squad of armed soldiers, their faces masked.

'Who is here with you?' they asked, as they moved into and around the apartment. She saw through the open door that other soldiers were flooding into the building.

Jasna told them that she was alone with her son Tibor. Her husband was in Norway.

Moving quickly, they searched each room of the apartment, and left.

'Close the door, and don't go out!' they barked, as they headed upstairs to another flat.

This was not to be the last that Jasna saw of soldiers, armed and in her apartment.

She had been kept in Mostar by an illness suffered by Tibor. A few days before they were due to leave for Zagreb, and then for Norway, he had woken with a red and swollen throat. By the time the day of departure had arrived, he had a serious infection and was forbidden by the doctor to travel for at least five days. Milan decided that he could not stay. As one of the few Serbs left in Mostar, he knew that he should go. He had packed a small bag towards the end of March, and with the papers necessary to take him to Norway in his hand, he was gone. He left on the day of an Islamic festival, with Mostar echoing to the celebratory firing of Muslim guns.

For every person living in Mostar in the early weeks of May, a similar story could be told. It was as if the breakdown of the alliance had been the final signal for total war to break out, with the last restraint removed. A wave of ethnic 'cleansing' was to leave Mostar one of the most desperate places of the whole Balkan crisis. Mostar, which had held out against this violence longer than most of Bosnia, was to become one of its worst victims.

Nikola and Sandra came back to Zagreb in early May to the news that things were worsening in Mostar. Two truck-loads of medicine for the city's hospital were waiting in Rijeka for delivery, and Nikola agreed to deliver one of them. Leaving Sandra in Zagreb, he arrived in Mostar on 8 May. The medicines delivered, he drove the empty truck out through the streets of the city. He could tell that there was a new tension in the air, that something was about to break. Even in the time they had been away, there had been a polarization, a separating of the two sides. People were visibly shocked to see the truck in the almost empty streets of the eastern sector. He left Mostar at around 5.00 p.m. on 8 May, just minutes before the streets were closed off by barricades dividing the two sides of Mostar. A few hours later, the city itself was shut off, and no one was allowed to come in or out. Sandra was relieved when he arrived safely back in Zagreb.

There was no question, in these circumstances, of an immediate return to Mostar. Stevo Dereta found a vacant apartment in Rijeka, and Nikola and Sandra moved in. They were to stay there, hostages kept from their home, for two weeks.

Nikola tried daily to contact members of the church, but was thwarted by a complete block in communications—no information was coming into or out of the city. He had no way of making contact. A breakthrough came with the news that Miro had been able to leave Mostar, and had set up a new base for Agape in Citluk, twenty-five kilometres farther south. Nikola telephoned him, asking him to find a place for them in Citluk or Medugorje. This would put them close enough to Mostar to get back into the city as soon as it was opened up again. But this possibility, too, failed, when they lost contact with Miro. It was only much later that they learned Miro had had to move again, to set up an aid office elsewhere.

The compulsion for Nikola and Sandra to return to Mostar was overwhelming. They had come from Spring Harvest inspired and encouraged. Thousands of British Christians, it seemed, were praying for them, and for the people of Mostar. But their work was now halted—no one even knew if they would be able to get back into the city at all. They were trapped, hundreds of kilometres away, and couldn't even find out if their friends were safe and well. There were, of course, possible alternatives: staying in Rijeka to work with Moj Bliznji, or setting up a new base in Zadar, halfway down the Adriatic coast. But they didn't even consider such ideas—it was in Mostar that they had married, and already they thought of it as their home. And their new friends, the struggling, infant church of the city, needed them.

'We need to know, at least, how things are in the city', Nikola said, when the frustration of being so far from home grew too much, 'so that at least we can decide what is the best thing to do. Without news of Mostar, we can do nothing.'

'Then we must go ourselves', Sandra answered, confirming the conclusion that he himself had drawn. 'If there's no way of contacting the church from this distance, we should try from closer at hand.'

They chose Citluk as the most appropriate destination, and set off, once again, into the war.

In Citluk they searched for Miro, but couldn't find him, and travelled on. Renting a room in Medugorje, they tried to get news of Mostar, but there was none. All they were told was that the situation was very bad, that the city was closed, and that they wouldn't be able to get in. But, remarkably, the news was different the next day. There had been a quieter night in Mostar; there might be a chance to get in.

They passed through the final checkpoint and saw the city spread out below the mountain road. Buildings were burning, there was gunfire and shelling. They knew at once that something terrible had happened, and was still happening, to their city.

'Be ready to lie down, if someone shoots at the car', Nikola said to Sandra as they worked their way down the steep approach road.

They sensed the danger as they came into the city, and knew that the sooner they could get off the road, the better. They went immediately to the Agape offices.

Incredibly, two of the women who had worked for Agape were there. This was the first day since 9 May that they had dared to come out of their homes. Both were gripped by fear, one because her husband was a Muslim and had not yet been found out. All around, the noises of war continued.

The son of one of the Agape workers came in to warn them that there was street fighting very close to the building, and to watch for snipers. The doorway to the office was in the direct line of fire, and it would be dangerous even to go out. Nikola stopped him as he was about to leave the office to zigzag his way to his home across the street.

'What should we do?' he asked

'Just go!' the young man said, terror and urgency in his voice. 'There is nothing you can do in these circumstances. Go, now. Get out of Mostar as quickly as you can.'

Sandra and Nikola accepted the cold logic of the young man's words. There was nothing they could do. They had nowhere to stay in Mostar: they had no keys to the one Agape apartment that they knew to be empty. The office, the very room in which, weeks earlier, they had held their wedding feast, was a snipers' target. The distribution of aid was rendered impossible. Miro had had to move out, and had sent Milan Pavicic, too, back to Zagreb. The warehouse, still full of food and supplies, was on the same side of the city but in a separate area now controlled by Muslims—with a frontier as real, and as dangerous, as the Berlin Wall. The

Cold War was over, the Iron Curtain gone, but other divides remained to haunt Europe from centres such as Mostar. Reluctantly, without conviction, they returned to their car and left the city behind them.

Stevo Dereta had been filled with concern from the moment Nikola and Sandra had headed south. He felt responsible for them, and could do nothing to help from such a distance. The news he had been able to gather of Mostar was frightening and disturbing, and he had been uneasy about them trying to get back.

Nikola telephoned him from Citluk.

'Stevo, the situation in Mostar is awful!' he said. 'We went back in, but there is fighting in the streets, constant shooting, and we have nowhere to stay. There's nothing we can do. We cannot go back.'

Stevo's honest reaction was relief. He had sent Nikola and Sandra to Mostar in the first place, and his concern for them was very high when people were dying there every day. The city was a dangerous place; they could only be safe if they were out of it.

'You've made the right choice, Nikola', he assured his friend. 'There's nothing else you can do.'

Nikola hung up the phone and looked at Sandra. They had driven from Mostar to Citluk in silence, hardly speaking a word, just looking every few moments at each other. In both their minds, the same thoughts were developing, coming into focus now as they told Stevo they could not go back. The two women at the office, gripped by fear, the other members of the church spread about the city, discouraged, afraid. They thought of the Muslims in the church, of the mixed marriages—people who would be facing, even now, the threat of separation and forced removal.

Sandra was the first to speak the words that both were thinking.

'We must go back.' Curiously, she had no fear. She just knew that they had to go back, that it was the only option, the only thing to do.

Stevo was surprised to hear Nikola's voice again, just half an hour after the first call.

'We've talked and prayed', he said. 'We've decided to go back to Mostar.'

'No, Nikola, wait', Stevo answered, his previous sense of relief evaporating. 'How can you go back when you were in danger even going in for an hour? What can you do?'

'We don't know what we can do', Nikola replied. 'We just know that we must go back. This is the time when we are needed most. Everyone is so frightened, they need our support.'

Stevo struggled to accept the decision, the burden of responsibility it brought back to him, and the fear he began to experience, even at a distance. But he could hear, even in the half hour since the first conversation, that there was a difference in Nikola's voice. Something had happened to produce this conviction, this certainty, against which there was no argument.

'We will pray for you both', he said. There was nothing more that he could offer.

Lidija Mackenzie reacted in the same way to the news. Asking Nikola to pass the phone to Sandra, she begged her to reconsider, to give the decision time.

'I know what we must do', Sandra replied, as firm in her conviction as was Nikola. 'We know that Mostar is where God wants us to be.'

'If you know that', said Lidija, 'then you must go.'

The couple shared a meal in Medugorje. The same day, they went back to Mostar.

Thousands of kilometres away, negotiations for peace were beginning to cross lines of compromise that had once been utterly rejected. President Clinton's influential negotiating team accepted, in late May, a new peace plan: one which left some of the 'ethnically cleansed' territories in the hands of their invaders. This had been expressly ruled out in every previous proposal, but was a recognition of the reality 'on the ground'. Even in Bosnia, it had been accepted, two months earlier, that the vision of a united, multi-ethnic state was dead, and that only co-operation, rather than co-habitation, was now possible. The new plan took harsh reality even further, recognizing that some of the burnt out, battered villages and towns of Bosnia would never be restored to their original occupants. Whatever the outcome of Bosnia's war, now just over one year old, it seemed certain that ethnic separation would be included. Hardly anyone now held out hope for the three races to be brought together again, or for any patch of Bosnian soil to be thought of as 'mixed'. The idealism with which the international community had once welcomed an independent Bosnia, the shortest-established country in the history of Europe, had crumbled.

Certainly, the forces in Mostar knew this to be true. And so, in common with their counterparts throughout Bosnia, they went on with their terrifying work of ethnic 'cleansing', to sort out the civilian population as coldly as a deep-sea fisherman might sort out his catch.

8

A Friendship Like *Melem*

*Virulent evil spreads through society like an
airborne disease; one cough infects a whole
busload. But the cure, like a vaccine, must be
applied one person at a time.*

Philip Yancey, 'Holocaust and Ethnic Cleansing' in *Christianity Today*

While Nikola and Sandra were dealing with the implications
of returning to Mostar, Stevo was at work developing the
vision of Moj Bliznji: a vision that was soon to run hand in
hand with the Mostar work.

In January, he had shared with friends in the United
States the dream of opening a Christian centre in or near
Rijeka, where refugees and others could be welcomed for
short stays, giving them the opportunity to recover from the
trauma of war.

'When I would go to the camps to meet refugees, and was
distributing aid from Moj Bliznji,' he later recalled, ' I always
asked myself how to break through their emotional problems:
how to help them in such a way that they might be enabled to
cope with these problems more successfully themselves.'

From the very first days of the aid programme, Stevo had
seen that the bare distribution of food and supplies was not
enough. The act of giving was doubled in value when it was
accompanied by words of hope and encouragement.

'Many people needed simply to know that someone cared
for them: that there was still a friend, somewhere', he said.
'Others needed to rediscover their dignity. They had lost
everything material—they needed to hold on to their identity
and worth.'

Stevo had developed, early on, a particular awareness of the needs of those caught on 'the wrong side': people of mixed race, or in mixed marriages, or simply living in the 'wrong' region. Thousands had suffered the direct blow of ethnic displacement, driven from their homes by violence—actual or feared. But there were also wider, deeper echoes of this violence, touching even those whose homes and bodies were unharmed.

'They need friendship, they need somebody with whom they can be themselves. Even on the surface you can see how many people are oppressed. They are afraid and don't know what to think. They have been forced to hide their identity.'

Stevo's early responses to these needs were simple and primitive. Seeing how humiliating it was for people to queue in the street to collect aid from the church, he would open the building, inviting up to 250 people at a time to come in. Sometimes he would share with them a few words of encouragement, urging them not to lose hope. Many of them told him how much this meant to them—more, sometimes, than the food itself.

'Your words are like *melem* to us', they would say. *Melem* is their word for an ointment put on wounds to aid healing. 'We have no one with whom to share our problems. Even if no one can solve them, it is good, at least, that someone listens.'

These early experiences had convinced Stevo that the offer of friendship in an atmosphere of Christian hope could help many whose lives had become desperate. He was eager to find a place where such friendship could be offered long-term.

The American friends, sceptical at first, were later able to offer funding. The question became one of premises.

In mid-May, Stevo was standing with a group of young people and their parents. The teenagers, for the most part refugees, had been taken, through Moj Bliznji, on holiday to stay with members of a church in Wales. Some, on their return, had maintained long-term friendships with their host families. One girl had been able to gain a grant to study in the United Kingdom, and would soon be living more permanently with the family she had first met on holiday. A group from Wales soon made a return visit, and when it came for the host families in Rijeka to say goodbye, Stevo was approached by Tomislav Latinac; it was his daughter who was to study in Britain. He reached out to shake Stevo's hand, but held it longer, looking into his eyes.

'Why do you love us so much?' he asked. 'It's not normal!'

Stevo searched for a satisfactory answer.

'You've probably heard that we are Christians,' he eventually offered. 'Because of Christ's love, we seek to love others as he did—unconditionally.'

'I have to tell you', Tomislav went on, 'that I have never, in my whole life, met such love.'

The two men began to talk together, and Stevo explained more of the work of Moj Bliznji and the church.

'We are trying right now to find a building', he finished, 'in which to establish a centre of reconciliation. We want to have a place where refugees can come, where we can help them restore their emotions and their lives.'

'I have just the place for you', said Tomislav excitedly, 'in Crikvenica.'

He described the small hotel, on the shores of the Adriatic, in a resort just a few kilometres from Rijeka. Like most of the tourist attractions on this part of the coast, it had been closed when war broke out.

The two men drove immediately to look at the property, and Stevo walked for the first time through the corridors of what would become, just three months later, a Christian retreat centre. In a beautiful, peaceful position, the 44-bedroom hotel had exactly the basic, no-frills facilities that the project needed. When Tomislav later came to check the contract, he confirmed that a seven-year lease had been signed, but dissolved, just a few days before his conversation with Stevo. They had talked at just the right time.

It would take several weeks for the paperwork to be processed and several more for the centre to be prepared, with volunteer labour streaming in from churches all over the world. But during the summer months, 'The Life Centre' was to become not only the all-consuming passion of Stevo and his team, but a vital part, too, of Sandra and Nikola's work in Mostar.

In Medugorje, a new Agape office had been set up. Nikola and Sandra phoned the secretary, and she came immediately to the restaurant they were eating in. She was alarmed by their plans to return to the dangers of Mostar.

'The warehouse is beyond our reach', Sandra explained. 'It is still full of food and supplies, but we can't get to it.'

'What about the Agape apartment, the one we were in before?', Nikola asked.

The secretary began to see that they were determined to go back, and realized that there was nothing she could do to stop them.

'It's too dangerous', she said. 'The fighting has been very heavy in that part of the city. Even if you could get to the apartment, it would not be safe to stay.'

They both knew that she was right. The apartment was a stone's throw from the Agape office, which they had already seen was unsafe.

'But there is the other apartment: where Miro was', she went on. 'It might be possible for you to have that.'

Back in Mostar a few hours later, Nikola and Sandra collected the keys from their new neighbours and moved in. Even for Sandra, who had spent hardly any time in the city, it already felt like the place where she belonged. For all the bombs and sniper fire, the couple were pleased and relieved to be, at last, at home in Mostar.

Their first task was to contact the members of the church. With the building shut down, these people had fled to their homes, and were not meeting anywhere. By visiting those they knew well, Sandra and Nikola were able to put out the news that the church was in business again. On the first Sunday after their return, they arrived to find a group already gathered outside the building, enthusiastic and grateful that there would, after all, be a service. About twenty people gathered for an hour, simply to sing, pray and share. It was only half the number who had been together regularly in March and April, but among them there were many dear friends.

They had already been delighted to find Jasna still in Mostar; Nikola and Sandra had thought never to see her again and their reunion had been one of joy and laughter. At church that day, another surprise was the presence of the Hudec family—Janos and Razija, with their children Vedran and Elizabeta. Nikola knew them already, but not as members of the church. They ate together after the service, and sealed a bond of friendship that was to take them through many trials in the months ahead, and lead, in time, to a bold and remarkable initiative for Mostar. The two women whom Nikola and Sandra had met in the office a few days earlier, Dragica and Marija, were also there. For many of those present, the same question was put to Nikola and Sandra:

'Why have you come back?'

The answer was to become the foundation of the church's work in the months that lay ahead.

'During the drive back to Mostar', Sandra explained later, 'all we could think of was Dragica and Marija in the office that day. They were gripped by fear. We knew that we could help them: we knew that it would be encouraging for them just for us to come here and to stay. Just by living in Mostar, we could be an example of what Jesus did by coming to Earth. We didn't have any expectations as to *how* we would serve; we just knew that it was right to be there.'

The simplicity of this conviction soon translated into strategy. The couple were keen to restart the work of the church if that proved possible. The aid programme, too, they would do all they could to continue. But their primary motivation was to support the Christians of this tiny community, and to offer friendship. Friendship, as it turned out, was the very *melem* that the open wound of ethnic conflict needed.

The ceaseless persecution engendered constant fear, for Jasna among others. Sometimes at night she would see the trucks waiting in the streets for the children and families. Even when it was hot, she would shut the windows—to block out the sound of crying.

One evening she was with Tibor outside the building, and the soldiers came with their trucks.

'Go inside your apartment, and stay there', they told them. They were clearing the street house by house. Jasna knew what was happening, because she had heard news from other parts of the city.

Jasna took Tibor into the bathroom. She washed and dressed him ready to travel. She knew that there would be no water or electricity on the other side. She knew, too, that the 'cleansing' was often accompanied by violence: that people had been killed on other evenings.

She told Tibor that they might have to leave, keeping him as calm as possible. In her heart, she asked God to keep them safe, to watch over their building and prevent violence from erupting.

But she was ready, if necessary, to go to the east, if that was what God wanted for her. Moments later, she heard knocking on the door. She opened to find not a whole squad of soldiers, but only one: a young man, unsure of himself.

'Is your husband here?' he asked.

Jasna told him the truth—that she was alone with her son.

'OK, thank you', he said, politely, and was gone.

Jasna breathed a deep sigh of relief, and with it, deeper still, a prayer of thanks. She knew from what she had seen from her windows, and had tried so hard to keep her son from seeing, that her fate could have been very different that night.

From May 1993 onwards, the 'cleansing' came in waves, area by area, throughout Bosnia-Hercegovina.

More and more Nikola and Sandra found that their purpose in Mostar was simply to be there for those who were targeted, and to accept all, regardless of race. They were determined that the church, tiny though it was, would be a place to which all could come, a pool of reconciliation in a spreading desert of hate.

Almost every day, the Christians would meet together: not in formal, church gatherings, but in one another's homes. They studied the Bible, prayed, and talked together. In the space of just a few weeks, they built relationships together that went deeper than many lifelong friendships; they were bonded together by common hardship.

'You have to understand', Sandra said, 'that no one could leave the city—no citizen of Mostar was allowed out. It was a hopeless situation. Each person had to choose: to take up arms and join the war, or sit by and wait, with no control over their own future.'

There was substantial poverty, too: most of those who stayed had no income at all. Officially, Nikola and Sandra were not seen as residents of Mostar, but of Zagreb, making it possible for Nikola to leave and re-enter the city with relative ease. This was a new beginning for the aid programme: no trucks, no warehouses—just a private car going out of the city to get food.

Later, when daytime electricity was resumed and phone lines were available, the Agape office became for many a link with the outside world; it also became one of the main suppliers of aid for the city, along with Caritas, the Catholic agency. Previously, there had been other, Muslim agencies, but these no longer operated in west Mostar. For the Muslims left in the west, Agape's was often the only door open.

Nikola and Sandra were overwhelmed by the growth of the church, both in numbers and in depth. People were converting to Christianity and immediately taking on the characteristics of lifelong disciples, for the intensity of the situation created a kind of hothouse for new Christians. Inspiration for the new church came directly from the pages of the Bible, and there were visible parallels with the first Christians of Jerusalem, of whom it was said in Acts 2:44–47:

'All the believers were together and had everything in common. Selling their possessions and goods, they gave to everyone as they had need. Every day they continued to meet together in the temple courts. They broke bread in their homes and ate together with glad and sincere hearts, praising God and enjoying the favour of all the people. And the Lord added to their number daily . . .'

Throughout this time, a pattern was emerging which was to become a foundational pillar of the church. There emerged a threefold commitment to serving the needs of Mostar.

The first commitment was to the feeding of the hungry. Along with Stevo, Peter Mackenzie and others, Nikola and Sandra had seen from the start that part of the church's mission must be to meet the physical needs of the suffering. *Serving* the people of Mostar in this way marked the starting point of their life in the city, and remained essential to it. It would later become one of the pillars of the charitable organization they would create. During daylight hours, before the evening curfew made it impossible to move around the city, they would move constantly in and out of the Agape office, taking food to different homes around Mostar. The programme was later to run on a much larger scale, as it had done before 9 May, but during Mostar's days of isolation, it consisted of one recently married couple, their private car and an office whose front door was often within the range of the snipers.

The second commitment was to the spiritual and emotional needs of the people of Mostar, and to see the growth and development of their church. Both Nikola and Sandra believed from the start that Mostar needed a church, and that the presence of an open, accepting Christian community could make a difference to the city. A place of reconciliation and forgiveness, the church could model a different way of living. At first Nikola and Sandra were tentative about this, but they became more and more bold as they saw how many people in Mostar were searching for just such a community. They initiated the chain of events by which the church grew, but the growth itself was, in essence, spontaneous. Along the way, the Mostar church became one of the fastest-growing evangelical churches ever seen in the Balkans, and one of the few known examples, in world history, of a church growing at the very heart of a war. Before long, the Skrinjaric bath was being used for baptisms and Jasna, among others, took this step to mark the depth and permanence of her decision to live as a Christian.

'Yesterday I put the old Jasna in the grave', she told her neighbours. 'Now I am new.'

The third commitment was slower to emerge, but in time it took its place as part of the foundation of the church. Day by day, Nikola and Sandra began to notice the effect that the war was having on the children and young people of Mostar. Deprived of education, of open spaces in which to play, of any sense of social norms, childhood was being eaten up by the experience of war. Like many people caught up in the Balkan crisis, Nikola and Sandra saw that young people were among the worst hit. Three years of suffering in an adult's life is hard to bear; but three years of suffering between the ages of thirteen and sixteen will leave a deeper scar, and for longer. The new church began to see that helping Mostar's young people should, and could, be a part of their mission. In time, it would become more than just a part. In the development of this third strand of their work, Nikola and Sandra moved parallel to, and later in partnership with, the growth of the Life Centre in Crikvenica.

In their early months, Nikola and Sandra had wondered which of these three paths they would find themselves following, but as events took over they found that they were walking all three, and that a church growing towards wholeness was the result.

Stevo, in turn, had hoped from the start that young people would be among those helped by the Life Centre.

His concern for the brokenness brought by violence to many lives was at its strongest when he looked at the young refugees whose lives had been so brutally interrupted by war. At Camp Hidroelektra, on the mountainside at Ucka, outside Rijeka, he saw how aimless and atrophied their lives became when they were stripped of all activity and support. And he knew, too, how many were nursing, in such terrible conditions, the emotional wounds of bereavement and terror; and how many had witnessed, in recent months, scenes that would turn the stomachs of those many years older. In all the areas touched by the crisis, there were children and teenagers growing up with a legacy of pain and hatred. For many of them, revenge had become the only language spoken.

As the Life Centre became established, the team working there were able to give long distance support to Sandra and Nikola. International contacts were put in touch with Mostar, and the flow of aid was assured once the city opened again. If Nikola and Sandra were the deep-sea divers on the dark sea-bed of Mostar, their air line went all the way north to Rijeka, and the Life Centre team manned the pumps.

In June, Nikola and Sandra were able to leave Mostar for a youth conference at Cakovec, north-east of Zagreb. Passing through Crikvenica, they were encouraged to hear that the Life Centre was soon to take shape. After the conference, they headed back to Mostar, travelling with friends who were visiting from Switzerland and the United Kingdom. At the final checkpoint before Mostar, frustration awaited them.

'Papers', said the guard at Nikola's window. His colleagues toured the car, looking in at every point. Nikola handed over the collection of passports.

'You cannot go into Mostar', the guard said, after a few moments.

Nikola knew instantly why: his friends, sitting in the back of the car, were carrying video equipment. For months, it had been impossible to get a video camera into Mostar.

'But I live there.' Nikola pleaded.

'I'm sorry', the guard confirmed, 'you will not be allowed into the city, unless you go in alone.'

Nikola had no choice. His friends had no transport of their own, and there was nowhere safe nearby for them to stay. He would have to take them back to the Life Centre.

The ten-hour journey north was one of frustration and disappointment, not least for the visiting team, who had hoped to meet the people of the Mostar church. What Nikola and Sandra couldn't know was that it would also be a journey of opportunity.

Exhausted from travelling, they decided to stay for a few days at the Life Centre, now taking shape in a building that had long been closed. They felt the deep, therapeutic effect of being in a place of peace, and a total contrast to the chaos they had been living through in Mostar. They talked with their visitors of the work of the church and, fresh from the Cakovec youth conference, of the needs of Mostar's young people. Quietly, under the soft, warm Adriatic breeze, they began to conceive of an idea whose boldness astounded them: an idea that would involve thinking the unthinkable and doing the impossible. It was only a seed but, once planted, it needed only time and plenty of watering to bear fruit. It was to result, just two months later, in the greatest blow that the church would ever strike against the isolation and desperation of Mostar, and in the opening of a door that, years later, still operates today.

Tragically, it was not merely video cameras that were prevented from entering Mostar in the summer of 1993. As the hatred splitting the city deepened, even aid convoys were blocked. Militia in Medugorje barricaded the path of UNHCR convoys, headed for east Mostar, as a terrible game of accusation and counter-accusation flared up between the Croats and Muslims of the city. People were dying daily, victims of both shelling and sniper fire. A single convoy was allowed through in August to deliver medicines to the hospital in the east; but those same medicines were destroyed four days later when the hospital took three direct hits in dawn shelling. The pounding of east Mostar continued, with thousands of people now besieged in the old city. In the streets on both sides of the front line, a new type of road sign, hastily painted on the walls of apartment blocks said: 'Danger, Sniper!' Homes began to suffer from the knock-on effects of shell damage: the loss of power and water. Children were called on to act as water carriers, running in zigzag lines to the standpipes to fill jerrycans.

In the British press, Mostar and Sarajevo vied for space as horror-stories from both increased. In Sarajevo, reporters highlighted the plight of the critically ill five-year-old Irma, who had developed meningitis after being seriously wounded in the mortar attack which killed her mother. The British Prime Minister intervened, and Irma and other critically ill children were airlifted to London to be found beds in the capital's hospitals. Meanwhile, thousands of other children, undiscovered by the spotlight of the press, carried their physical and emotional wounds.

Mostar itself slid deeper and deeper into the darkness. Even a cursory glance at the British press headlines of the day shows the sad and degenerating situation:

MOSTAR'S PLIGHT NOW WORSE THAN SARAJEVO
The Daily Telegraph, 19 August 1993

THIS IS THE END OF THE WORLD
The Independent, 23 August 1993

PEACE HOPES CRUMBLE LIKE MOSTAR'S BRIDGE
The Daily Telegraph, 25 August 1993

HUNDREDS MOB UN CONVOY IN MOSTAR
The Daily Telegraph, 27 August 1993

The headlines were the bullet-points of a dismal, agonizing history. On the streets, the terror of shelling and snipers was complemented by hunger and the ongoing scourge of ethnic 'cleansing'.

But the headlines showed only one side of the story: the dark side. Even in this deep night of trial and fear, a Golgotha for the people of Mostar, there was the gentle promise of resurrection. In the infant evangelical church, a growing number of people were finding faith in a God of miracles, a God alive enough and close enough to hold them through the night. Asked at this time why she and Nikola chose to stay in Mostar, Sandra spoke not for them alone, but for all the Christians in the city.

'God has done something so deep in our hearts', she said, 'that we do not feel the fear.'

The headlines proved that war was bringing out the worst in humankind. The Mostar church, with a quieter, less publicized voice, declared the simple truth that God was bringing out the best. In the summer of 1993, Mostar lived through its crucifixion night; but there was also something beyond—its resurrection morning.

9

Mostar, *Moj Grad*

We're going where the sun is shining,
We're going where the sea is blue.
We've seen it in the movies,
Now let's see if it's true ...

Bruce Welch and Brian Bennett, 'Summer Holiday'

MOSTAR, SUMMER 1993

One single idea was growing steadily as Sandra and Nikola returned to Mostar, with neither visitors nor video equipment. Its ingredients were simple. In the north, Stevo and his team were preparing an old tourist hotel to welcome refugees desperate for a place of peace. In the south, the young people of Mostar were living through the hell of war with no sign of relief. In the hottest city of the Balkans, summer can be oppressive even without shelling and sniper fire. What if a holiday in Crikvenica could be offered to the young people of Mostar?

'It's impossible', Sandra said to Nikola for the fourteenth time. 'Even the adults are not allowed out of Mostar. How will we get papers for teenagers to leave?'

'I don't know', said Nikola, 'but we should at least try. Stevo says the centre will be ready at the end of August. They're saying here that they will open the schools again on September 6th. We've just got time to take a group for a week.'

The initial idea was to take children from the families already in the church, or closely linked to it. When they talked it through, they saw that they could take perhaps twenty-five young people. They phoned Stevo.

'You'll have to hire a coach', he said, 'and that will seat

fifty. You mustn't waste the spaces, or the opportunity. Could you find twenty-five more?'

'We can try', Nikola replied, without really knowing how.

No more than twenty-five young people could be contacted through the church; it was time to talk directly to the Mostar authorities.

At the Centre for Social Care, Nikola met Andelko Matinovic, who took immediately to the idea. In all the time of war in Mostar, nobody had offered anything to the young—and those who were responsible for their care were glad of every opportunity to help them.

Andelko introduced Nikola to Marko Bevanda, Director of Services, and the three people agreed a plan. The church would use twenty-five of the available places while the social services would take the other twenty-five, sending the young people in their care most deeply affected by the war. Domestic breakdown and violence had not stopped in Mostar just because there was a war on, and many young people were living in problematic situations. What the war had done was to bring to a standstill most of the efforts to help them.

Andelko agreed not only to help set up the holiday, but also to accompany the group for part of their time away. For months, he had occupied himself with keeping track of the 300 orphans formerly in his care, and he knew that a group of twelve had been placed not far from Rijeka. The trip north would give him the opportunity to visit them. Marko, too, agreed to travel with the group, essentially to verify the standard of care offered by the Life Centre. Finding fifty young people, however, was only the beginning of the story. It would also be necessary to gain permission for the trip from two separate authorities in two completely different parts of the country.

The first was the military government of west Mostar, whose militia were manning the city's checkpoints, and without whose permission nobody could leave or enter. Nikola went to see their chief administrator, nervously explaining the idea and giving detailed histories of the

Mostar church and of the Life Centre. Much to his surprise, the response was positive.

'Bring me the name and date of birth of each person involved', the administrator instructed, 'and we will issue papers for the whole group.'

'Does each of them need to come in and apply?' Nikola asked, anxious to get the paperwork absolutely right.

'That won't be necessary, just bring me the names.'

Nikola began to see a door opening. What had been impossible just a few days earlier was becoming not only possible, but likely.

Permission would also be needed, however, from the Croatian government in Zagreb. The Croatian Ministry for Social Care was cracking under the weight of the huge refugee influx. Already over-burdened by those fleeing the first war, mostly from the Krajina, it was unprepared for the later flood from Bosnia. In late 1992, it had pleaded urgently with other governments, particularly in Europe, to accept more of the thousands of families still streaming out of the war zones. To give muscle to this plea, the government had ruled that no one would be allowed into Croatia without papers proving that they had access to a third country. They would accept refugees in transit, but to refugees without papers, the borders were officially closed. The result was that complicated papers were needed for all non-Croats to cross into Croatia. These could only be issued by the Ministry in Zagreb.

Three times Nikola and Sandra travelled to the Croatian border to establish which papers they would need, to be sure that they would not be turned back. Three visits, and three different answers later, they knew that only direct permission from Zagreb would guarantee their safe passage. The office in Zagreb, however, was inundated with requests, and there were delays of some weeks in issuing papers. The application was sent through Stevo, who added a statement confirming that the young people would stay for just ten days at the Life Centre, after which they would be driven back to Mostar.

The authorities in Zagreb responded only by saying that if permission were granted, it would be communicated directly to the border crossing. Nikola left the matter in the hands of the Life Centre team, and waited for news.

A coach company was found in Medugorje, the lists of names were compiled, the permission from the military government was issued, and everything was in place except permission from the Croatian government. Twenty-four hours before the planned departure, there was still no news from Zagreb.

'We should phone the Life Centre, ask what is happening', said Sandra.

'I can't', Nikola said. 'I just can't do it. If they say no, now, when all these kids think their holiday starts tomorrow, I don't know what I would do.'

'So what are our options?' Sandra asked. 'Do we cancel the holiday?'

'No', Nikola said, firmly. 'We can't. We must try. If we phone, and the answer is no, we will be breaking the law by going. But if we haven't had an answer either way, we can at least try . . .'

He didn't make the call.

They didn't dare broadcast a rendezvous point for the coach, for fear of offering too easy a target for snipers or artillery. Instead, by word of mouth, they told the young people to be in the vicinity of the cathedral the next morning, ready to board the coach at the main bus stop when it arrived.

Parents crowded around Nikola and Sandra, taking the address of the Life Centre, asking questions, giving information about their children. Almost all the teenagers had been able to get to the departure point, along with Nikola, Sandra, Andelko and Marko. They boarded the coach with excitement and expectation. Some had not slept at all the night before, such was their anticipation of getting out of Mostar, and of seeing the sea again.

They passed through the first military checkpoint and slowly climbed the hill out of Mostar, passing under the site-lines of the guns that still pounded the city. A second checkpoint posed no problems, and they drove quickly to the border with Croatia. No permission, however, had been sent from Zagreb: there was no record, at the crossing, of a planned trip by a coachload of teenagers.

Nikola had become, in just a few months, a seasoned veteran of border crossings. He had learned one simple rule: whether you have the right piece of paper or not, hand over every piece of paper you can find. He gathered the identity cards and, from those who had them, passports, together with the papers issued by the military administration, and those issued by the social services, naming all the children in their care. He gave the entire pile to the military police officer manning the border post, who immediately went to the caravan serving as an office to telephone for advice.

Twice he tried to make the call, and twice he couldn't reach his superiors. He came back to the coach.

'It's OK, just go through', he said, handing Nikola back the piles of paper.

The coach moved forward, changing up through its gears, heading north to the Adriatic coast. It had been a little over two weeks since Nikola and Sandra had begun planning, in earnest, for the trip, still wondering if it was possible. They could hardly believe that it was now happening, and wondered, now, how they would fare in their new-found role as youth workers.

CRIKVENICA, AUGUST 1993

The Life Centre opened for business on 22 August, after a mammoth effort of cleaning and preparation by a team of volunteers. The first group of visitors were from Camp Hidroelektra, a spartan refugee camp on the mountainside at Ucka, just outside Rijeka. The camp was home to 400 Bosnian Muslims, mostly women and children. Of these, eighty were able to spend ten days at the Centre.

From the very beginning with this first group, the future role of the Life Centre was evident and established. In a place of peace and, compared to the wooden huts of Ucka, comfort, there was an immediate impact on those who came.

Many had arrived saying that revenge was their only reason for living.

'The first chance we get,' they would say, 'we will kill.'

All of them had been driven from their homes. Some carried photographs of houses they now knew had either been destroyed or handed over to the families of their enemies. Many had witnessed terrible atrocities: their mothers or sisters raped, and then killed before their eyes; columns of children and old people, some sick and wounded, driven by fear over the mountains; families who had previously lived in self-built, beautiful homes, who were now searching in the rocks and scrub for caves in which to shelter. All these people had suffered bereavement, separation, or both. Most of their male relatives who were over eighteen, whether sons, brothers, husbands or uncles, were lost to them. Some had been killed, others were fighting in front-line battles, and others still had been taken to camps from which rumours came of the most appalling conditions.

Many of the women on the camp were hardly able to eat—not for lack of food, which came in from humanitarian groups, but because of their overwhelming grief. They spent their waking hours in tears, their minds filled with thoughts of the husbands and sons they had lost. The younger people, for their part, seemed empty and directionless, burying their grief under a false cloak of indifference. Stranded in a camp on a deserted mountainside, without transport to visit even the nearest town, they had passed their time smoking, inventing war games, and keeping their tears at bay. Camp Hidroelektra was, and is, a clear illustration that, for the refugees of Bosnia, the grief, as much as the homelessness and hunger, must find its cure.

But after only ten days at the Life Centre, there was a visible change in many of these families, a rebirth of hope. After their stay, many people had found the time to put their thoughts down by writing letters. The problems and stresses of living as refugees did not go away, but many said they felt better able to cope. A man who had witnessed the rape and murder of his mother spoke for many in the group.

'This has been a ten-day miracle' he said. 'I feel released from the hatred and anger.'

Within hours of opening its doors, the Life Centre had found its vocation.

The ten-day stay of the Mostar group was less traumatic, but no less valuable. The young people had no fixed programme; instead, they relaxed together, enjoying the sea, walking in the town, and building new friendships. On their final night, a Christian rock group played, and the Life Centre became a youth club. Andelko's twelve orphans also came for the evening. Throughout the concert, the young people chanted:

'Stevo... Stevo..., Nikola... Nikola..., Sandra... Sandra...'

The three leaders had become heroes in their eyes, winning their loyalty through simple warmth and affection. Neither Nikola nor Sandra had any training or experience in youth work, nor even models to work from. In the pre-war churches of Croatia, there had been little or no formal work amongst the young beyond the provision of a Sunday school and occasional youth meetings, often highly religious and ritualistic. The experience of forty-three lively teenagers for ten days together was a baptism of fire. Nikola and Sandra learned their youth work directly from the young people themselves!

There were also tears, particularly on the night before leaving. One girl celebrated her sixteenth birthday on the last evening of the holiday. She spoke to Sandra with tears in her eyes.

'I don't want to go back to Mostar', she cried. 'I've lost so much there. So much of my childhood was happy, but now it is gone.'

The previous year, she had celebrated her birthday in the absence, already, of friends who had left as refugees. With the small group that remained, she had talked of her sixteenth birthday, a year away, dreaming that those friends would be back. But when the day had come, no one was back, and even more had left. Her best friend, a Muslim girl who had lived in her street, had been forced to go to the east side of the city. They had completely lost contact.

'Today is the birthday I dreamed of,' she said to Sandra, 'but where are the friends I have lost?'

The purpose of the holiday was recreational; it was not to be an overtly 'Christian camp' as such. Such activities as were organized were only social, with games and some singing. But a significant number of young people made the choice, nonetheless, to become Christians. By the time their coach re-entered Mostar, the church had a new youth group, and Nikola and Sandra had new jobs.

Both Andelko and Marko were pleased and impressed by the care shown on the holiday. They saw Nikola and Sandra, despite their lack of training, as gifted youth workers. Andelko, a veteran of thirty years in the care of children and young people, saw something in the couple that he had never before experienced.

Before they had first arrived at Crikvenica, on the long coach ride north from Mostar, Nikola had explained to Andelko that their approach to youth work would include a spiritual dimension and that they saw spiritual education as part of their task. This had surprised Andelko at first, since he had been used to evaluating youth work by more material criteria, in a system that denied the existence of God. Any form of religious education was forbidden, by law, to children in the care of the state. But after the holiday, when he had seen the ease with which Sandra and Nikola talked with young people, and the enthusiastic response, he began to think more deeply about their approach.

'Perhaps we have been wrong, all these years,' he said to Nikola, 'to deny in our work the spiritual dimension.'

Andelko's passion for the young came partly from his own history. Born in Mostar in 1938, he was the eldest son of a working-class family, his parents, too, Mostar born. At the age of seven, he saw his father shot by partisans—they came and took him from his home, and killed him before his entire family. The sole reason, as far as Andelko knew, was that he was Croatian. Being the eldest of four, Andelko began to help his mother to care for the family. But an anger had been born in him that day which, even now, he finds it hard to deny. But with it came a concern for children and young people cut off from their families. He studied philosophy, and taught Croatian, before joining the social services.

At the Mostar Children's Home, he was responsible for 135 children, living in seven family groups. He found himself acting as a surrogate father to many of those in his charge. Many of them had no one else to turn to.

'They told me their small secrets', he said to Nikola. 'They had no one else. I would teach them how to behave, as a father takes care of his children. I was their spiritual father.'

When war broke out in April 1992, there were sixty children present in the home, on which thirty-seven shells fell. They moved, with the staff, into the basement. Three of the children were wounded during the first few days of war—two by sniper fire and one by shrapnel. Andelko himself came close to death when a shell exploded four metres from the desk at which he was working. The force threw him to the floor. When he recovered, he found that the desk was peppered with shrapnel—the wood itself had saved his life.

He was able, over the next few days, to arrange placements for the children, some in Croatia and some in Skopje, in Macedonia. A military helicopter airlifted the last group from the city.

Andelko felt bereaved when the children had gone, as if a part of him had been taken away. It became his mission, almost an obsession, to keep track of them and ensure their safety. His dream was to bring them back to Mostar. Many were physically well cared for in the places of safety that had been found for them; but they spoke, all the same, of coming home.

Listening to this caring, committed person speak of the lost youth of Mostar, with tears never far from his eyes, Nikola understood again the importance of 'home'. *Moj grad*, meaning 'my town', was a phrase spoken with great feeling by those who came from Mostar. How it mattered not only to be in a place where death does not threaten, but to be in a place of belonging!

'I love Mostar', Emilija had said when asked if she wanted to leave the city. 'Mostar is my home—*moj grad*. Everything I know is here.'

On the return journey from Crikvenica, the coach gained four extra passengers. Spring Harvest had agreed to extend their fund-raising for the youth work for a further year, and had sent a film crew to the city. They met up with Nikola and Sandra at the Life Centre, joining them on the last two days of the holiday, and they travelled south with them.

Nikola was nervous as they approached the Mostar checkpoints. This was not the first time he and others had tried to take video equipment through. On this occasion, however, they were allowed to pass without incident, and as the coach descended the long, steep hill, the air resounded with the cheer of the young people.

'Mostar . . . Mostar . . . Mostar!' A further cheer went up when they saw that electric power was on below.

Yet as they came into the city, three huge explosions shook the coach. Serb shells were coming in, and the Croat response was coming out. It was evening, just minutes before curfew time. In the gathering darkness, tracer fire made huge arcs of light over the town. On the ground, the night was filled with the sharp, repeated crack of sniper fire.

Fortunately, the coach reached its destination unharmed. The teenagers tumbled off the coach excitedly to meet their parents, bubbling over with news from their holiday. In the half-light of a summer's dusk, warm and balmy, the animated crowd of young people and their parents unloading luggage from the coach might have been anywhere in the world. Families reunited, friends said goodbye. These were moments of near-normality in a city long since driven into chaos. The holiday had been a great success.

While the young people had been away, however, there had been heavy shelling of certain areas, and some people came back to hear that relatives or neighbours had been killed. For all the relaxation of a youth holiday, they were still residents of a city at war. Emilija Jupek explained how it felt to return to such a place:

'We were glad to be coming back to Mostar because we had not seen it for ten days. But when we saw the city, that the shooting and shelling had not stopped, we wanted to be back in Crikvenica, where we had been safe.'

Out of the effectiveness of the holiday, Nikola and Sandra began to see new possibilities for the work of the church in Mostar, and in Bosnia. Their church now had the only Christian youth group in Bosnia-Hercegovina, and they had seen how openly the authorities welcomed their involvement with the young. No one else, it seemed, had time for young people. Their social and recreational lives were suspended by war, their parents were taken up, day by day, with the struggle for survival, in some cases the struggle to get out of Mostar. No schools had operated since May, though the plan was to reopen them in September. Clearly, there was a need for ongoing, permanent youth work. Nikola and Sandra had always seen that the church could be a place of reconciliation, a community in which all were welcome and in which forgiveness and love overcame the power of hatred. Now they saw that young people, too, could be brought into such a place. By offering shared

117

recreational facilities to young people, they could bring them into the experience of reconciliation, and out of the trauma of war.

Through the work of Spring Harvest, they had come into contact with Youth for Christ, the worldwide youth mission agency whose British workers were heavily involved in the Spring Harvest youth programme. Talking through their experiences of the holiday with their friends in Youth for Christ, it was clear to Nikola and Sandra that something new was beginning. If hope was to be reborn in Bosnia, they asked, where else could it be reborn but amongst the young? If a simple ten-day holiday could make such a difference, how much more effective could a long-term programme of youth work be?

A decision was taken immediately to increase the church's involvement with young people, and to replicate, in the future, the holiday experience. From the British side, it was agreed that funds would be found for the purchase of a minibus, to aid the work with young people and children, even if that simply meant driving them safely to school or church. Within two months, Nikola had taken delivery of the vehicle.

Prior to the war, there had been four evangelical congregations meeting in Bosnia-Hercegovina; for the most part these were small, and none had a formal youth programme. Nikola and Sandra's work had brought new growth and young people to the only one of those churches which was still open. They began to see that their threefold commitment, to aid, to church growth and to the young, was more than an accident. What they were seeing was the emergence of a new model of what it means to be a church, not only in wartime, but in the post-war nations that would emerge.

Placing their hands, together, on a map of Bosnia, and praying with the team that had come from Spring Harvest, they committed themselves again to service, to hope, and to reconciliation; and they wondered how far-reaching the impact of their new work might be, both in Mostar and further afield. The answer, when it came, was to be beyond their expectations.

There were still surprises to come in the adventure of Mostar's newest church, but there were also trials ahead. For the church, November and December 1993 were to bring the toughest days they had yet lived through together. Indeed, 10 November, was to be, for the city, perhaps the lowest point since the nightmare had begun.

10
Bridge Keepers of Mostar

On the banks of the playful Neretva lies a town
of unequalled beauty—
a harmonious link between oriental and
western architecture.

Photo-guide to Mostar, Turistkomerc, Zagreb

UNITED KINGDOM, NOVEMBER 1993

British journalist Robert Fiske sat mesmerized by the images unfolding on his television screen. Ten, twenty, thirty times he rewound the short video tape and watched again, horrified. The tape was poorly filmed, shaky, and slipping in and out of focus. But its contents were chillingly clear: it showed in gruesome detail the destruction of the Stari Most bridge. Writing of the tragedy in *The Independent on Sunday*, Fiske described the last moments of the bridge's life, as seen on video:

In its last milliseconds of existence, tank shells smash into the west side of the parapet in a cloud of brown dust. Then the entire sixteenth-century bridge—'a rainbow rising up the Milky Way' as a traveller to Mostar described it 400 years ago—falls in a slow, lazy way into the waters of the Neretva to be met by a majesty of spray. Press the rewind button and you can rebuild the bridge, the spray falling back into the gorge, the old Turkish stones rising mystically upwards to recompose themselves in their magical span.'

The horror felt by this one journalist, who had passed many times through Mostar, in peace and in war, was shared by people all over the world. For many, the pounding to destruction of the Stari Most bridge constituted the city's darkest hour. In the real Mostar, far from the comfort of video recorders, there was no rewind button. The bridge, once fallen, was lost.

When Nikola first arrived in Mostar, in December 1992, the city was still graced by the elegant Stari Most. When Sandra joined Nikola three months later, she, too, visited the bridge. Peter Mackenzie, recalling earlier visits, always remembers the bridge at the very heart of the town. No one, it seems, could visit Mostar without visiting the Stari Most.

A government tourist guide, published in 1985, describes the bridge in its pre-war beauty:

In the entire course of the Neretva, from its source to its mouth at the Adriatic Sea, Mostar is the spot where it is at its most beautiful. No one, neither chance visitor nor tourist, can but admire the perpetual beauty of this wonderful example of Turkish architecture. It is the bridge which became Mostar's symbol, which carried its name not only through Europe but throughout the world.

To many people, the Stari Most was Mostar. Its keepers of centuries ago, the Mostari, had given the city its name. Its single span arched high above the gorge of the Neretva, whose blue-green waters swirl with life. Before the war, the children of the city—Croat, Muslim, Serb—would delight in leaping together from the bridge's centre into the cool waters far below. The bridge was held together, at its construction in 1566, by a mortar made from eggs and goat's hair. It had survived war and earthquake, invasion and celebrity to live its four centuries unshaken. Its architect, the celebrated Hajrudin, had seen his first design collapse, and had been threatened by the sultan with death if the second followed suit. In fear for his life, he fled the city moments before the scaffolding was removed, leaving a monument to his skills which was to outlive him ten times over.

When war came to Mostar, the Stari Most became newly significant. For the previous twelve months, it had been the only one of the city's seven Neretva crossings to remain intact. Crudely covered by a shaky tin roof, and swathed, in its last days, in old car tyres, it had been the final, tenuous link between the two sides of the city.

Symbolically, the Stari Most linked East and West. For centuries, the Neretva Valley was the border between two cultures, between Western Christianity and Eastern Islam. Mostar was the favoured crossing point, the meeting of two worlds. The steep gorge across which the bridge stretched was more than a river, it was the divide of two world-views, a cultural fault line. For many of the city's residents, especially among the younger generation, its survival was a token of hope.

Strategically, the Stari Most was also the last, slender link between the 50,000 Muslims trapped in east Mostar and the western banks of the river. Too dangerous to use in daylight, the bridge became, each night, a desperate passageway from the main Muslim enclave in the old town to the small area of the western city centre still held by the Bosnian army—and the most fiercely contested section of the front lines.

On the afternoon of 9 November, the bridge became the target of mortar and tank shells. The tin-roof helmet and car-tyre flak jacket were effective protection against bullets and shrapnel, but useless against direct bombardment. The bridge was badly damaged, although it held, mortally wounded, to live through one last, crumbling night. Early the next morning, a further thirty-three shells found their target, and the ancient stones of the Stari Most gave up their fight, ending 400 years of history.

'They pounded it on Monday afternoon and then again this morning', said one official who visited the city the same day. 'It fell into the river at 10.30 a.m. There's nothing left. There were grown men walking around the city with tears in their eyes. It wasn't a symbol of the Muslims or the Croats. It was a symbol of the whole city.'

Stevo remembers the shock he felt when he heard of the shelling. On Monday evening, Croatian television news had carried the report that the bridge was shelled, but intact. The next evening its destruction was announced.

'I felt that this was one more sign,' Stevo said, 'one more thing of destruction, nonsense destruction. It makes you ask, why? How far? When is it going to stop? I was sorry, not so much for its historical value, but for these people: now even their bridge has gone. These are ordinary people, who don't want war, who pay the highest price. Something is gone which belonged to these very ordinary people.'

'Those people who destroyed the Stari Most: they didn't have a soul!' said Andelko Matinovic.

Sandra remembers the reactions of young people to the bridge's loss:

'People were very emotional about the Stari Most, especially the young. They had lived together, had enjoyed going out into the old city. The bridge symbolized togetherness, harmony, access to the city centre.'

The emotional symbolism attached to the bridge, its role as the last link across the ethnic fault line of the Neretva valley, and its architectural value all gave its destruction a historic significance. No one was killed in the shelling, or even injured, but the loss of the bridge drove cruelly home the despair of this beautiful town, and the insanity into which its people had fallen. On 9 May, the Croats and Muslims of Mostar, formerly linked in an alliance to defend their city, had begun to shoot each other. Close neighbours had become sworn enemies and vent their wrath on one another across a front line in places less than one metre wide. Exactly six months later, in the desperation of their anger and violence, they showed that they would destroy even the treasures of their own city if they had to, so deep was their hatred. It was as if the war was a virus, eating the city itself, like antibodies short of external enemies to fight that turn inwards to destroy their own cells.

The shock waves sent around the world by the shelling of the bridge were keenly felt, too, in the Mostar church; 10 November came to prove a turning point in its work.

For both Nikola and Sandra, the autumn had brought its own trials and struggles. It had also, however, seen many encouragements, despite all the ravages of war. The success of the youth holiday brought an enormous boost to the life of the church. Many of the young people began to attend regularly, some bringing with them their parents and other relatives. A calendar of youth meetings based at Nikola and Sandra's home was added to the church's programme. Nikola had been reluctant to invite young people to the church building itself, because its neighbourhood was still very dangerous, and once the Skrinjaric home had been identified as a base for youth meetings, it was rarely empty, whether a meeting had been planned or not. The door remained permanently open, and the house became Mostar's unofficial youth centre.

The church was now made up of about fifty people, but was growing weekly, if not daily. Janos Hudec proved himself an able organizer in helping in the administration of aid. Not long into 1994, the church found itself responsible for feeding almost half of west Mostar. Janos also brought to his work not only management skills but an irrepressible sense of humour, and he was liked by all.

However, the threat of Janos and Razija's family being forced out of west Mostar remained. She and Janos found it to imagine where a Hungarian-Muslim family would find their place an ethnically-divided Mostar. Like many mixed families, they feared that, even in peace, this city would never again offer them a place of security.

The only solid hope, in this sea of fear, was the church. The growth of the church, the aid programme, and their friendship with Nikola and Sandra gave both Janos and Razija a new, deeply rooted confidence, until they began to live *despite* the war raging around them. At times, the church would gather in the Hudec home, for prayer and Bible study meetings, or simply to be together. Those less accustomed to life on the front line would sometimes run to the window when shells were heard, to see where they fell. The eleventh-floor apartment commanded a panoramic view of large sections of the city's most disputed streets.

'Leave them be,' Razija would say, 'forget the war. They have their job to do: we have ours.'

It was not an easy task, to forget the war, but in the new church, for moments at a time, it was at least possible.

Like many of the newer members of the church, this family had an immediate impact on their neighbours. A capacity to stay spiritually afloat, when so many other people were drowning in despair, drew curiosity, interest, and questions. Janos and Razija were responsible for introducing a number of relatives and friends into the church, and several of them stayed.

Among these were Esad and Zvjezdana Dedic, the family who lived in the same block, their east-facing windows bricked up. Theirs, too, was a mixed marriage, and they lived with the same fears and insecurities as their neighbours. Zvjezdana's father had been born in Mostar, her mother in Zadar. In 1983, she had married Esad, a Muslim, in Mostar. When war had begun to shake Yugoslavia, they had not believed that it would come to their city. Living in one of the most mixed communities in Bosnia-Hercegovina, they thought they would be spared. They enjoyed a good life in Mostar, and thought they would go on doing so.

'But we were wrong', says Zvjezdana, bluntly.

Their daughter Jasmina was born in May 1992, just weeks after the outbreak of the first war. Zvjezdana gave birth in the basement of the hospital, sheltering there from the constant shooting. By the time Jasmina was celebrating her first birthday, the second war was just four days away. Esad, serving as a Muslim in the Croat military police, had to manage the tensions of ethnic division more than most people.

When the Dedic family joined the church, Jasmina became the star of the meetings and services, interpreting the singing in her own playful style and, as her confidence grew, dancing in the aisles. She was a favourite both of the church's older members, and of the teenagers. Walking to and from church, she would hold the hand not of her mother or father, but of Vedran, Janos and Razija's teenage son. In far less happy circumstances, however, she was to become the focus of the church's desperate prayers before 1993 ended.

Sadly, among the growth and encouragement, the autumn brought conflicts of an unexpected nature. Even in the desperate circumstances of war, the spectre of church politics could not be kept entirely at bay. The month of October became a time of testing and trial for the Skrinjaric family.

The rocket-like growth of the church, and its involvement with young people, had not won the universal approval of those who had been in the former Mostar evangelical church. Legally, the new church was simply a renewed version of the old one, but Nikola and Sandra's leadership, and the programme they had adopted, had never been formally ratified by the denomination, based in Osijek. This had not seemed to matter when membership was small, but it became significant as the church grew. When opposition arose from the small minority of those who had been members of the former church, the questions grew painful and complex.

In January 1993, when Nikola had come back to settle in Mostar, the church had been closed, and its people, for the most part, were scattered. The building, in one of the areas of east Mostar most heavily bombarded by the Serbs, had been utterly destroyed. The belongings which some of the members had hurriedly stored, for safety, in the church basement were lost under the rubble: the site was too dangerous to approach. When a new congregation began to gather on the west side, a handful of members from the former church joined them, fast becoming committed to Nikola and Sandra's leadership. These few, now members of the new church, did all that they could to negotiate between the couple and those who wanted them to leave. The negotiations were only partially successful and in October the church had to leave the Agape building, losing its meeting place and separating, for a time, from the aid work.

This became one of the most memorable times in the church's history, as they met, for just over a month, in homes rather than in a central building. Just as in the months before the summer, when meetings had taken place almost daily to protect the Muslim converts from forced deportation, so now there was an acceleration in the building of relationships. The loss of the building led to a deepening in the commitment of many, and new members continued to be added to the group. Jasna's home became, once more, a focal point for the church, and the location for many meetings. Growth continued, despite behind-the-scenes tensions.

Well away from Mostar, in both Zagreb and Osijek, Peter Mackenzie became involved in the controversy over Nikola and Sandra's work. Over many years, he had built positive relationships with many church leaders in all the denominations. He took it upon himself to plead the case for Nikola and Sandra.

One of the unique features of the Mostar project was that it brought together Baptists and Pentecostals. The Moj Bliznji network was Baptist, but Sandra and Nikola had come into it from Pentecostal circles. Their work in Mostar was linked with an evangelical church through a Pentecostal group, and with Agape, the Pentecostal aid agency; at the same time, it continued to be supported by Stevo, Peter and Moj Bliznji, all Baptist, and to work closely with the Life Centre. Deep friendships undergirded these partnerships, but they were nonetheless unusual: church unity had not been a prominent feature of pre-war Yugoslavia. It was Peter who approached the Pentecostal leadership in Osijek.

'Nikola and Sandra are the people who God is using in Mostar', he said to the Osijek leaders of the evangelical churches. 'If you don't back them, you're going to lose the whole project.'

His words were dramatic, but accurate. Nikola and Sandra had never been formally-appointed leaders of the Mostar church, but there was no question, in fact, that they were leading it. After several weeks of confusion and difficulty, the

Osijek group decided on the only workable solution, and it made a choice that was to give new confidence and hope to the church.

Inviting Nikola and Sandra to Osijek in October, they ordained Nikola formally as the pastor of the Mostar church, and re-commissioned the couple for their task. In the same, simple ceremony, Peter Mackenzie was also ordained, so that he could be free both to preach and to baptize in Pentecostal churches. He became one of the few ministers in the Balkans ordained in both Baptist and Pentecostal denominations. Nikola, who had come to Mostar just ten months earlier as a truck-driver, became the recognized minister of the Mostar evangelical church. This was a development which neither he nor Sandra had foreseen but, when it came, it seemed the natural thing to do, and they welcomed the formal recognition of their work. The ordination gave them the opportunity to reunite the work of the church with the work of Agape. It also allowed Nikola, a little later, to have something which turned out to have its uses. Visiting England in January 1994, he mentioned to a Methodist minister that his ordination had not included the issuing of a clerical collar. On the spot, the minister removed his and passed it on.

'If you don't mind the second-hand variety,' he said, 'you're welcome to it.'

The collar more than served its purpose later, easing Nikola's way through checkpoints, and through his various meetings with the authorities.

The agreement which had served to provide the building for the former evangelical church was, by then, null and void. The search was on for new premises. Some promising options presented themselves, but came to nothing, until Nikola was approached by someone who had been a regular client of the Agape warehouse and had seen Nikola as someone whom he could trust. He passed by the Skrinjarics' house one day, and was amazed to see a stream of young people going in. Nikola explained something of what had been happening with the church, and how the summer holiday scheme had come about.

'Maybe I could do something for you', the man offered. 'Maybe there's something we could work on together?'

'Our greatest need, right now,' Nikola said, 'is for premises. We need a place to meet, and to base the aid programme.'

'I think I can help you', he said.

Two days later, a new home for the church had been found, and legal permission for its use as a church building had been arranged through a friend who held a senior position in the military administration. The building's ground floor had housed a service centre for electrical goods and was littered with debris, from old televisions to broken glass; but it was available for as long as its former owners stayed away from Mostar. Many buildings in the city centre had similarly been vacated by their owners and were under the supervision of the army. The new building was just a few hundred metres from the site of the former church, and was still close to the front line areas. The experience of singing worship songs to the accompaniment of sniper fire would not, for this church, be over yet.

The whole church joined in the cleaning programme, and within two weeks the place was ready. Sandbags were piled to ceiling height outside the windows, with makeshift polythene double glazing added inside. A crude cross was marked on one wall with packing tape: the only religious symbol in the building. A few weeks later, a new aid programme was launched from the premises, once more under Janos' care. The ex-workshop was to serve as the church, office, warehouse, youth centre and venue for wedding receptions well into 1994.

Nikola's ordination, the new premises and the re-registration of Agape all contributed to a boost in the church's confidence. War still raged all around them; east Mostar remained under siege; the peace process was lurching forwards, but slowly, with month-long periods of stalemate and silence; fear still ruled the city, as the front lines were hotly contested and occasionally broken; the shelling continued; whole streets remained out of bounds to civilians, ruled over by snipers; and the process of ethnic 'cleansing' went on. But for all this, there was an atmosphere of peace and joy in the church. New people turned up constantly, drawn in by the changes they had seen in friends and neighbours, and the church continued to carve out, in a divided and divisive city, a multi-ethnic community, open to all.

The destruction of the Stari Most on 10 November brought, at first, discouragement and shock to the new church of Mostar. But strangely enough, it did not set the church back. Instead, it served to galvanize its vision for the future.

'People were very emotional when the bridge fell, and they began to talk of the good old days', Sandra explained. 'As we thought about it, we saw that we should turn from our emotional attachment to the past, and think more of the future. The question that mattered for Mostar was: what is going to happen now?'

'The old history of Mostar was destroyed when the Stari Most fell', added Nikola. 'Now a new history had to begin for the city.'

Sandra and Nikola began to believe that their task in the church was to build a new spiritual and emotional bridge, bringing former enemies to reconciliation and peace. The loss of the Stari Most seemed to be the final, desperate act in killing the old Mostar and it was appropriate to have a time of mourning. But now the church needed to look forward, and discover what part it could play in the rebuilding of the city.

It was in the aftermath of 10 November, thinking these issues through, that the idea was born to establish a charity, in Mostar and in the United Kingdom, to give long-term support to Nikola and Sandra's work. Committing itself to the core values of *Service, Hope and Reconciliation*, Novi

Most, meaning 'new bridge', was to be the vehicle which would carry forward the church's threefold mission of aid, church growth and youth work, channelling the efforts of Christians into the reconstruction of Mostar. In time, it was to lead to a long-term contribution to the rebuilding of Mostar, and the creation of Bosnia's first Christian youth and community centre. In the wake of three years of division and destruction, such a centre would offer a place in which all were welcomed and in which reconciliation, forgiveness and peace were possible.

At the time, of course, there were no such concrete plans in mind. In November 1993, as the stones of the Stari Most settled into their new location under the Neretva's waters, the people of the church felt only a sense of longing for a new direction and for a better future. The words of sixteen-year-old Emilija Jupek captured the feelings of many others at the time:

'Yes, it bothered me, when the bridge fell,' she said, 'but it bothered me more that so many young people were being killed. The bridge is not as important as young people's lives.'

If the old bridge was a symbol of architectural excellence, a treasure from the past, then the new bridge, the 'Novi Most' that the church was to build would be a symbol of hope for the young: a reconstruction not of stones and mortar, but of young lives.

Ironically, other areas of the world in which violence and hatred had become the norm were experiencing, just at this time, the new green shoots of peace. After years of terrorist attacks and vengeful reprisals, Israel had agreed on 9 September 1993 to recognize the Palestinian Liberation Organization. Four days later, the world's press converged on the lawns of Washington's White House to witness one of the decade's most significant handshakes, between Israel's Yitzhak Rabin and the PLO's Yasser Arafat. 'Shalom, Salaam, Peace', ran the headlines of the world, as the two men began to work towards a full peace accord for December 1998.

Not long after, the possibility of peace in Northern Ireland also grew when a historic agreement was signed in London, in December 1993. It was to be months before the accord was to have a substantial effect on the ground, but the wheels of peace were moving forward.

South Africa, too, was moving slowly away from the violence and division of Apartheid when parliament voted, in December, to end white minority rule.

Tragically, this worldwide wave of peace eluded Bosnia. The fighting went on, with thousands dying in trouble spots around the country, and new atrocities every day. In Sarajevo, 1,300 shells fell on Christmas Day 1993, despite a holiday cease-fire.

In Mostar, several street cafes reopened in November, their owners somehow judging that the loss of the Stari Most marked the beginning of the end of the war. The terrace of the ironically-named Phoenix Cafe just metres away from the church, was crowded with new customers when a shell came down, arcing high above the surrounding buildings to land directly in front of the cafe. A teenage girl was killed. Mostar, in November, was still living through the darkest of days.

Slowly but surely Nikola and Sandra, and with them the church, redirected their hope towards the building of the new bridge. But Mostar's war was far from over, and for the church, the toughest trial was yet to come.

11
Jasmina's Story

This is not the children's war.
The children are not responsible.

Emilija Jupek, Mostar

MOSTAR EVANGELICAL CHURCH, DECEMBER 1993

'The first victim of war is truth', said Winston Churchill. There has been ample evidence in Bosnia to prove his words right: the control of information has been a primary part of battle.

But if truth is the first victim of war, the second, hard on its heels, is childhood. Of all the casualties of battle, children are the hardest hit. In cities under siege, it is they, seeking in their playful innocence to run in the open streets, who may be the snipers' most common victims. Parenthood, at the best of times a complex task, becomes a nightmare in wartime.

Sunday, 12 December was a typical winter day in Mostar. The city rarely experiences low temperatures, except in late January, and the winter sun was as warm as it can be during an English spring. One hundred people had gathered for the church's morning service, crowding into the converted television workshop. Forced by numbers to use two adjoining rooms, the church sang songs shown on the wall by two overhead projectors. The singing, as always, was enthusiastic and emotional. From the very start, singing had been part of the life-blood of the church, providing an almost therapeutic communal activity.

When the service was over, the congregation spilled out happily into the square in front of the building. Sheltered on all sides by high-rise apartment blocks, they felt secure, even though they were just two hundred metres from the front line. The back windows of the church, protected by sand-bags, looked directly onto wasteland, at the other side of which was the front line. To stand for too long at that side of the building was dangerous; but here in the square there was safety—a haven protected from snipers' bullets.

As always, little Jasmina Dedic had danced unsteadily throughout the singing, and played noisily during the quieter moments of worship. Her round, olive-skinned face and soft curls framed large, inquisitive brown eyes. She was loved by all and she knew it. Her family had been in the church only a few weeks, but they were old friends of Janos and Razija Hudec, and had quickly been integrated into the new community. The service this morning had been refreshing and joyful, and the two families talked and laughed as they walked across the square towards their block. Esad had been on duty, and would be waiting at home.

Vedran, Janos and Razija's fifteen-year-old son, took Jasmina's hand and walked with her behind the adults, coaxing the youngster with the incentive of the waiting Sunday lunch: a promised feast of humanitarian aid, as always. In the 100 metres of road between the square and the apartment, Jasmina's tiny legs slowed the pair down, and the rest of the group had already gone inside by the time they approached the block. Zvjezdana, Janos and Razija were at the entrance to the building; Esad was already upstairs in the apartment.

They say that the most deadly instrument of war is the sniper. From a distance well outside the victim's range of vision, the snipers' telescopic sights can find their targets, following every movement. One squeeze of a trigger extinguishes life. More people have died at the hands of snipers than from any other cause in the Bosnian wars. In Mostar, 1993 might well have been called the year of the sniper. The city's residents had therefore developed a complicated code of behaviour to dodge the bullets, bypassing areas visible to hostile forces or running zigzag across exposed intersections when no alternative was possible. Even inside apartments, where windows were vulnerable, a circuitous route might at times be necessary just to cross a room. On outside walls, the warning 'Danger, Sniper!' became a common piece of graffiti, hurriedly applied in huge white letters. By mastering simple rules and by respecting the danger of the sniper's bullet, a citizen of war might hope to live to see peace.

Against shells, however, there is no such defence. There are no rules. Numerically, shelling has caused fewer deaths than sniper fire in Bosnia; but the deaths that shells have caused have been random and unpredictable. There is little warning, and no effective counteraction. And when the sounds of war become a daily aural backdrop, the mind grows used to them—although it still distinguishes, subconsciously. In the few seconds available after the ear has detected the eerie whistle of a shell close by, the mind's computer works frantically to assess the direction of travel, the likely point of impact, and the type of shell. In most cases, the computer is too slow, and the damage is done before even half the questions have been answered.

The shell attacks on Mostar were varied, but there were broadly three types of missile. The first, the old style, would climb and fall in a rainbow-like arc, exploding on impact. The second, more sinister type followed much the same predictable arc, but exploded before it landed, spraying shrapnel over a wide area: buildings or bodies up to one kilometre apart were often damaged in this way by a single shell. A third type of shell was less common; it climbed a high arc, easily clearing surrounding buildings or defences and, from its highest point, it would then drop almost vertically. In Mostar, where many streets were blocked on several sides by high-rise buildings, this type of attack was lethal. Streets that 'felt' safe could become, in one attack, as vulnerable as an open plain. There was no defence, except to stay permanently huddled in a bomb-proof shelter, or to live somewhere else. Neither of these options was open to the population of Mostar in 1993.

Walking slowly into the shadow of the twelve-storey block, Vedran and Jasmina felt as safe as they ever had. No shell had ever fallen on this sheltered stretch of road.

The adults inside the building knew, seconds before the impact, that the shell was coming, and that it would hit close. They had no time to know anything else. Janos and Razija had already started up the stairs; Zvjezdana, in the entrance, was the closest to the children.

It came in high, over the rooftop of the block, and fell sharply, landing a little more than a metre behind Vedran and Jasmina. A huge explosion, followed by a vicious spray of shrapnel, sent both children to the ground. Zvjezdana spun round, startled, to see Vedran lying in a pool of blood, screaming and trying to get up. Jasmina lay, silent, beside him. She ran to scoop Jasmina into her arms, fearing for one terrible moment that she was dead. She was overwhelmed with relief when her child began to cry.

Holding Jasmina close to her body, her eyes were fixed on Vedran, who was covered with blood. She knew that he would need to be taken to hospital, and turned immediately to run for Esad, who could get the car.

Esad had heard the shell approaching, then the blast. He had run to the seventh floor window in time to see Vedran lying on the ground: a tiny figure, oddly shaped. He saw his wife standing beside the boy, but didn't see Jasmina, who was hidden in her mothers arms. Turning quickly to leave the apartment, he leapt down the fourteen flights of stairs three or four at a time, and ran out into the sunlight, towards the wounded boy. A few steps behind him, Janos followed.

As Esad and Zvjezdana met, he heading towards Vedran, she towards the building, she instinctively placed Jasmina into his arms. It was then, for the first time, that she saw blood on her own hands and realized that Jasmina, too, was wounded. She was bleeding heavily from the back of her head.

They fetched the car, and hurried both children to the hospital at the southern edge of central Mostar. There was no traffic, and Esad drove fast, reaching the hospital in just two minutes.

The emergency team examined both children, and took X-rays, particularly of Jasmina's head. They were concerned and preoccupied; no one stopped to explain, to the anxious parents, what was happening. In time it was established that Vedran had been hit by twenty-four separate pieces of shrapnel. None had penetrated deeply, and all were removed. It transpired, later, that the shell had landed in a patch of soil which had slightly softened its impact, and reduced the spray of shrapnel. Had it hit concrete, at such a distance from the two children, the results would have been far worse. Vedran, who at first had seemed the hardest hit, was unhurt but for the cuts and bruises.

The anxious group waited one and a half hours for further news of Jasmina. They had no idea why it was taking so long, until the doctor came to them.

'Your daughter is seriously wounded', she said. ' She needs to be examined by a brain specialist as soon as possible. We are arranging for transportation to take you immediately to Split.'

Jasmina lay on a stretcher, conscious but disorientated. Her mother softly stroked her cheek.

The ambulance sped out of Mostar, with Esad and Jasmina on board. Zvjezdana was by now in a state of severe shock, and stayed in Mostar. Driving at breakneck speed, they reached Split in just under two hours—for Esad the longest two hours he had lived through. Not long out of Mostar, Jasmina had lost consciousness. She was pale and cold, as if all the blood had already drained from her.

'Is she dead?' Esad asked the nurse, as machines were connected to her tiny body.

'She's unconscious, but holding on', the nurse assured him. Moments later, he asked again, 'Is she dead? She seems so cold.' He desperately rubbed her cheeks, willing life into her little body.

By the time they had reached Split, Jasmina had slipped into a deep coma. The doctors came out from the hospital building to meet her straight from the ambulance and speed her inside. They connected her to more machines, and took a CT scan of her brain. At last they were able to explain to Esad what was wrong. The prognosis was not good.

Two tiny pieces of shrapnel had punctured the back of Jasmina's neck, just below the skull and had sunk twelve centimetres into her brain, lodging just behind the forehead. Externally, the bleeding had stopped, but the brain itself was still bleeding and there was nothing that could be done to stop it. If it didn't cease, she would die.

The doctor tried to encourage Esad: 'There is a chance, just a small chance, that your daughter will live', he said. 'But we won't know for six or seven days. If the bleeding doesn't stop, there's nothing we can do—it will only be a matter of time before she dies. If it stops, there may be hope.'

'What about damage to the brain,' asked Esad, anxiously, 'if she does survive?'

'There's no way that we can predict her condition', the doctor replied. 'She could be anything from severely impaired to fully normal. Until she's past this first crisis, we won't know.'

Esad didn't know what to do. Zvjezdana was back in Mostar, waiting for news. He had relatives in Zadar, closer to the hospital, but telephone communication was almost impossible. He decided that he must speak with his wife. Leaving Jasmina, unconscious, in the care of the Split hospital, he headed back to Mostar.

Zvjezdana had tried for two hours to get through by phone to Split, but could not get a line. Although she suspected the worst for Jasmina, she refused to give in to her fears. Jasmina had been such a happy child, so carefree and lively. Just hours earlier, she had been clapping and singing in the church. This could not be the end of her life.

Friends from the church began to gather at the apartment, to encourage Zvjezdana and to wait, with her, for news. By the time Esad returned, at 8.00 p.m., a substantial crowd had filled the home.

Esad reported the doctor's comments, exactly as he had heard them. Zvjezdana began to cry. She had hoped for better. The news that came was closer to the worst. For all they knew, their daughter might already be dead.

'All we can do now is pray', someone said.

The idea was strange to Zvjezdana. She had only been in the church for a few weeks and was still learning the very basics of what it meant to be a practising Christian.

'I have no faith, and I have no hope,' she said to Nikola, 'except what you have taught me. We can do nothing to help Jasmina, and neither can the doctors. Nothing else is left for us: a miracle is our only hope.'

'This is when we need to know', said Nikola, gently, 'that Jesus can make miracles happen. This is when it matters that he has done so in the past, and can do so again. We must pray, and wait for the miracle.'

There was no narrow triumphalism in all this: Nikola was as desperate, as shocked, as everyone else. But the church had made a commitment, publicly, to a God who made miracles happen. When the crunch came, it had to believe it, or quit.

They prayed that evening, and agreed to meet at three the next afternoon, and at three every afternoon until a breakthrough came. Nikola was able to get news of the crisis out of the city, and churches in Britain, America, Germany and Croatia began to pray, some at 3.00 p.m. each day.

In Mostar, the prayer was simple: that Jasmina would come back to the church, 'lively and jumpy', as before.

After just three days, there began a change in Jasmina's condition. The bleeding stopped, earlier than had been expected. She came out of the coma, and was taken off the hospital machines. She was transferred to an ordinary bed in the children's ward. After a further seven days, Nikola was able to drive Esad and Zvjezdana to Split to visit their daughter. She recognized her mother immediately, calling out 'Momma' as she came close. Just two days earlier, her grandfather had visited from Zadar, and she hadn't known him.

Her progress was remarkable. The doctors still feared the possibility of brain damage, and kept her closely observed, waiting for the right moment to take a second scan.

'It's not all over yet', they said to Esad and Zvjezdana. 'Sometimes in these cases there is a period of apparent recovery, and then, quite suddenly, there can be a relapse.'

Back in Mostar, those who had committed themselves to pray every day at three continued to do so. Their agreement was to pray until the day Jasmina came back to Mostar. Their prayer was the same, simple plea: that she would come back as healthy and as lively as before. The chain of prayer around the world continued.

Zvjezdana moved to her family's home in Zadar, so that she could visit Jasmina every three or four days. Jasmina said nothing to her during the brief visits, but hugged her tight. She had not yet stood since the accident, and it was to be a month before she spoke. Christmas was celebrated at her bedside, with presents of chocolates and soft toys brought from the church.

On the first day of 1994, Jasmina was released from hospital, to be taken to Zadar for ten days of further rest. She was still barely mobile, and uncharacteristically quiet. It was the return to Mostar that completed her healing.

As soon as she re-entered her home, she began to run, play and talk. Her brother, with whom she had constantly played in the past, was on the receiving end of an endless stream of kisses. She saw her sister, her grandmother and grandfather, and ran to each in turn. Within minutes, it was as if she had never been in hospital. The return coincided with a visit to Mostar by a team from Youth for Christ. Hearing that Jasmina was back, visitors and church members alike converged on the family home. With moist eyes, Esad and Zvjezdana recounted the events of the past weeks, and thanked those at home and abroad who had prayed. With

Jasmina playing at their feet, the group offered together prayers of thanksgiving and joy.

Shortly afterwards, Jasmina made her first visit to the church since her accident.

'Just as we had prayed', Zvjezdana recalled, 'that she would come back lively and jumpy, like before: that's how she was. It was wonderful, miraculous.' The three o'clock prayer meetings stopped.

At the time this book was written, Jasmina was still well, and appeared to be developing normally. The doctors have prescribed anti-epilepsy drugs, as a precautionary measure, but she has shown no sign of fits. She will be kept under medical observation for some time. She still carries the shrapnel in her brain.

It would be foolish to make rash claims about Jasmina's recovery or parade her as 'Exhibit A'. All anyone knows is that that Jasmina had little chance of living, and every chance of dying, but returned, six weeks later, to dance in the church. She is a miracle child simply because she is alive. Between her departure and her return, a group of Christians, most of them newly converted, gathered each day to pray for this lovely child. Why she recovered, when so many others in Bosnia have not, is part of the mystery of God. No one knows why such oases of mercy and joy should be granted in so vast a desert of suffering. But for those who longed for Jasmina's return, it is a source of immeasurable gratitude and joy. They can but be thankful. For Vedran, in particular, who at fifteen had wrestled with a dark sense of responsibility and guilt, it was truly wonderful to have his tiny friend alive again.

The dark days of fear and hope, when Jasmina lay deep in a coma, forged a deep bond among the Christians who prayed for her. In a sense, the Mostar church came of age during this time, just as many families do when faced with the possibility of such a loss. The church emerged from the crisis stronger, more deeply united, and awed at the wonder and mystery of God.

Sandra had been deeply moved by Zvjezdana's plight—a mother fearing the loss of her child. Jasmina had been born into one war, had lived through a second, and had almost died. Not long before the shell had fallen, Sandra had discovered that she, too, was now pregnant. She couldn't help but wonder how safe would be the Mostar into which her first child would be born.

It is not only the children directly hit who suffer through war. Bereavement, displacement and trauma also come to rest, in times of conflict, on other shoulders far too young to bear their weight. Ten-year-old Gabriel and his mother, Irena, had lived through two years of such trauma by the time they joined the church in the summer of 1993. Irena was Croatian and, by then, a single parent.

Before the war, Irena and Gabriel Mikulic had lived with Irena's parents in the village of Vrapcici, a few kilometres north-east of Mostar. In November 1991, when Serb reservists in the village began shooting, Irena feared for the safety of her son, and fled the village. Her mother and father, two uncles and their wives all stayed. She and Gabriel stayed in Split, gathering what news they could of their family. In June, the Serbs retreated from the village, and she was able to go back. Her mother and father had disappeared, and her uncles too. The house was empty, but intact; it had been occupied by JNA troops. Two months later, Irena's mother's body was found. It was to be another year before she was told that her father, and both her uncles, had also been killed. Unwilling and afraid to stay alone in the house, she returned to Split, where Gabriel had a place in school.

In June 1993 she came to Mostar itself. Leaving Gabriel with friends in town, she went out to clean up the house. Gabriel had asked to see it, to know that his old home was still there. On 27 June, they celebrated Gabriel's tenth birthday and, two days later, they went together to the house. Gabriel was happy and playful, thrilled to be home, asking neighbours to recount their stories of the past months. Their peaceful return lasted less than twenty-four hours.

'The next day was 30 June,' Irena explained. 'Early in morning, 3.15 or 3.30, we were woken by shooting, explosions, grenades. We got up. It was dark but lit up by explosions. We didn't know what was happening, only that it was war. Gabriel was so shaken I had to hold him so he wouldn't fall.'

Within twenty-four hours, the Bosnian army had come to round up all non-Muslim civilians. They were held together in a basement, then boarded onto a truck, which headed out of the village.

'Where are they taking us?' asked Gabriel.

'I don't know, son', said Irena, fearing the worst. The truck headed towards the same rubbish dump where, months earlier, Serb troops had taken local Croat and Muslim people and slaughtered them, creating mass graves on the spot. Irena held her son close, and they sang together, afraid to look where the truck was going.

When it stopped, they had passed beyond the dump, and were outside the prison in east Mostar. They were held for one month in the prison, where 200 people shared one blocked toilet, and water and food were scarce. Gabriel fell ill, and it was only when they were transferred to a disused primary school outside Mostar, that he began to improve. In their two months as prisoners, there were days when they were well fed, and left in peace. Other days, however, brought hunger, bullying, and distress. More than once, Irena stole bread from the guards' kitchen to feed the prisoners' children. Twice they were offered freedom in a prisoner exchange, but twice the exchange fell through. They had been taken out of the prison and driven, blindfolded, through the battle zones, only to be brought back.

At the third attempt, in September, they were taken by car to the front line. There was no guarantee of safety, and there was the constant threat of sniper fire. In the back of the car,

Irena told her son what to do, where the lines were, and where to run to if she was shot. They were taken through the Muslim lines, to a Croat-held village six kilometres north of Mostar. There they were freed. The next day they walked, across the mountain, into Mostar.

They were allocated an apartment in Mostar, because Irena's father had been killed, and they soon became enthusiastic members of the church. Irena, too, wanted to train in youth work; Gabriel re-entered school, and made new friends; and a Muslim family were given the freedom to live in their house in Vrapcici. Irena and Gabriel never lost the habit, forged in times of fear, of hugging one another often. They don't know what the future holds, nor if they will regain their rightful home—but in the context of Mostar's war, in autumn 1994, they were glad to be alive.

Irena and Gabriel were just one of the many families to join the Mostar church during 1993 and 1994. Indeed the church gained new members almost constantly during this time. There were also, in the midst of growth, goodbyes. Not long after Jasmina's recovery, Janos and Razija and their children finally emigrated to Australia in May 1994. They had contributed remarkably to the growth of the church, and had been valued and loved by its members. They had also, quite by accident, set in motion a project that would live on in Mostar long after their departure, for if Nikola and Sandra were the conceptual parents of Novi Most, it was Janos who provided the concrete to build it.

Novi Most came into being in 1994. Janos had been talking with Nikola, not long after joining the church, about the different roles he had enjoyed in Mostar before the war. He had been an industrial economist, and found himself elected president of the Communist Party in his sector of Mostar.

'I wasn't even at the meeting', he joked to his new-found friend. 'They nominated me, voted, and elected me all in my absence. Next meeting I turned up to, I was president!'

He had also been on the management committee of the Mostar Judo Club.

'The what club?' Nikola had asked

'The Mostar Judo Club,' Janos had repeated. 'We had the best results in Bosnia-Hercegovina, and the biggest club. We had classes for every age group. It was one of the most popular youth activities in Mostar.'

'Where did the club meet?' Nikola asked, intrigued.

'We had our own place, in the town centre,' Janos said, 'not far from the new bank. It's ruined now: blown to pieces. Only the walls are still standing. It's still ours, though. We were the only sports club in Bosnia-Hercegovina to own the freehold on our own premises.'

Neither man knew, in the innocent triviality of their conversation, how significant this judo club was to become.

12

Hope for the World

The weight of our undoing will bring us to our knees.
The groan of expectation is the whisper of the trees.
Renewal is a healing thing,
A healing thing.

Jon Birch, 'Hope for the World'

MOSTAR: EAST AND WEST, SEPTEMBER 1994

Nikola clutched the scribbled note, searching for street names in the derelict remains of the old town. Twice he asked directions, but to no avail. It proved impossible, on this first trip, to visit Alesa.

He crossed back into west Mostar deeply moved by what he had seen in just two hours in the east, and was determined to return.

A few days later, he was more successful, finding Alesa and his family shaken, but in good health.

'What do you need most?' Nikola asked them, after two hours together. 'What can the church do to help you?'

'We have no fuel for the winter', Alesa replied. 'We don't know if we can survive the next four months without heat.'

A week later, Alesa's wife was able to cross into the west, to collect heaters donated by the church.

'For our brother and sister in east Mostar', Nikola said to Sandra, remembering that it had been heaters that had first brought him to Mostar. 'Now the church is on both sides.'

The discovery of Alesa and his family, alive and well after twelve months under siege, brought encouragement and fresh challenge to the church. It was a reminder that for many in Mostar suffering was still very real: the church had a role to play in both west and east.

Throughout 1993, the progress of peace in Bosnia had seen several false starts, hollow promises and bitter disappointments. Each time one party was willing to sign an agreement, at least one of the other two would refuse. Months went by without progress, for all the globe-trotting of the negotiators. But things were changing, slowly. As 1994 opened, peace did seem closer, and painful compromises had been reached about obstacles which, months earlier, had seemed immovable. Like a bar room brawl, the fighting that the negotiations had failed to stop had slowed down from the sheer exhaustion of the combatants. There wasn't much left to destroy in Bosnia. The signing of the Washington Accord in February was the biggest step forward in the struggle for peace, and it soon began to have an impact in Mostar, under European Union supervision.

The church itself had continued to grow throughout the new year, as did the scale of its work. Karmelo Kresonja moved into the city in early 1994 to direct the work of Agape; his wife, Ivon, was a teacher and was to join him in July. Friends of Nikola and Sandra's from Zagreb, Karmelo and later Ivon were a welcome addition to the church. Alongside the aid work, they were also gifted pastoral workers, and began to share the load in the running of the church. Ivon gained approval from the local education authority to run Christian education courses which were to be based at the church, but linked in with local senior schools. Two other helpers, Ljerka Simunkovic and Klaus Domke, joined the Agape team and boosted the work of the church.

As Mostar edged slowly towards peace, the question of premises once again became crucial for the church. The agreement for the use of the television workshop would end as soon as the former owners were ready to return to the city—an inevitability once peace was established. With plans for the church and its youth work to expand, there was a need for more than just a meeting place on Sundays. The solution, as unexpected as it was comprehensive, came through Janos, and his role with the Mostar Judo Club.

Janos was a person whose open enthusiasm and warmth consistently touched those around him. By February 1994, most of his fellow directors of the judo club had, through his influence, joined the church. They were deeply impressed by Nikola and Sandra's approach, and enthusiastic about their dream to expand their work with young people. The judo club had been one of the largest youth activities in pre-war Mostar, and its directors were committed to continuing its work. In March they came to Nikola with a proposition: they would sign the club premises over to the church if the church could raise the funds for its rebuilding. The only condition was that the judo club should be able to continue to operate from the building, alongside the church's programme. The agreement was to be for forty years.

At the same time, the new charity, Novi Most, was being formed in Britain, to provide ongoing support for Nikola and Sandra's work. Created by Youth for Christ with the endorsement of Spring Harvest, the charity became operational in May 1994, employing a full-time UK director, Paul Brooks, in July. Registered charity status was given later in the year, with Lady Catherwood agreeing to be the organization's president. The Catherwood family had strong connections with wider Europe through Sir Frederick Catherwood's role as vice-president of the European parliament. They also had close friends in the former Yugoslavia.

Novi Most adopted the strengths already evident in the work in Mostar as its core values: service, hope and reconciliation. The rebuilding of the judo club, to provide Bosnia's first Christian youth and community centre, along with the training and resourcing of youth workers, became the charity's first priorities.

Throughout this time, the church's direct work with young people was growing more significant. A visit in

February by TVB, a musical project of Youth for Christ, enabled the church to offer a concert to Mostar teenagers, the first such event since the outbreak of war. The Washington Accord had just been signed, but had not yet brought peace to the city's streets, making it too dangerous to hold the concert in Mostar itself. A hotel was booked in Medugorje, and seventy people, mostly teenagers, were brought the thirty kilometres from Mostar, to join an audience which included several UN officers.

The members of TVB, all young themselves, were apprehensive of the visit to Bosnia, and especially to Mostar itself. Each member of the group had the choice to stay behind in Medugorje, but in the end they all made the journey into the city on the Sunday after the concert and were deeply affected by their participation in the service. Like all those who have gone into Mostar to identify with the Christians there, they immediately sensed the feelings of joy and hope that were evident in this fledgling church in the midst of pain and suffering.

The visits to the city by outsiders had great significance for those who were essentially its prisoners. One visitor commented:

'I thought at first that responding to the invitation from the Mostar church would not be worth the risk. I couldn't see what difference it would make. By the time I left, I knew that just being there, a Christian among Christians, was significant. It demonstrated to the young believers that they were part of something bigger: there were those on the outside that cared.'

To people trapped in a city rotting with the cancer of war, the simple companionship of outsiders coming in was, at times, a lifeline. During the February trip, it was confirmed that two experienced staff from Youth for Christ in Britain would move to the former Yugoslavia, to help train and equip youth workers and make that lifeline stronger. Andy and Helen Harrington and their two young children, along with Amanda Smith, moved in the autumn of 1994.

The work of the Life Centre also expanded in 1994. With the hotel converted and operational, the group was offered a second building—a run-down villa two kilometres along the coast at Selce. The villa had been a drug addict's squat before the war, and desperately needed refurbishment. It was handed over to the Life Centre team in the spring, and was transformed in a large work programme run by volunteers, to reopen in the summer as a youth hostel and camp. Full from the very first day, the villa welcomed up to 200 young people at a time, throughout July and August.

The Novi Most minibus became a regular shuttle, taking a total of 135 Mostar teenagers up to the villa to join the ten-day camps. Each group had an adult chaperone from the Mostar church, drawing a wide team into the youth work. The teenagers were, again, deeply affected by times of refreshment and emotional renewal. Many returned to Mostar having committed themselves to serve others in the city.

The experience confirmed for Nikola and Sandra that youth work was essential to the programme of the church. The plans developed well for the youth and community centre at the old judo club in Mostar, the aim being to serve the physical and spiritual needs of the city's young people all year round, in a way that holidays could only achieve occasionally.

The Skrinjaric family itself grew in 1994. Nikola and Sandra's daughter, Viktorija, was born on 2 May. Sandra escaped the intense heat of the city to spend the summer months at the Life Centre. Nikola visited regularly, but even so, Sandra missed Mostar and regretted the decision to be away for such a long time. She was glad to return.

In September, their first Sunday together again in Mostar was both moving and significant. Many of the threads of the church's recent history were brought together that day. To begin with, the morning meeting in the converted television workshop was also a service of dedication for Viktorija. She was the first child 'presented' in this way in the church, just as her parents had been the first couple married. The congregation of 130 had already gathered by the time Sandra walked in with Viktorija, to be greeted by cheers and applause. On this occasion, as always, singing formed a significant part of the service. There were many tears on faces deeply lined with recent pain, as the congregation sang:

'And now, let the weak say I am strong, let the poor say I am rich, because of what the Lord has done for us.'

In a simple act of dedication, Nikola and Sandra, on this day not church leaders but parents, stood with their baby at the front of the church while their friends gathered around them to pray. As in every community, the 'rites of passage' celebrated in the church strengthened its bonding and identity. Viktorija reminded the Mostar church of their commitment to one another as a family.

Then, with the service still in progress, Nikola was called out, and slipped quietly into the office. The architect given the task of redesigning the judo club had arrived unexpectedly, and wanted to talk with him. He had finished the initial drawings, and handed Nikola thirty pages of detailed plans—the first stage in the transformation of the site.

At the evening service of the same day, there was another interruption of cheering and applause. Anita and Drazen, the second couple ever to marry in the Mostar church since the outbreak of war, had returned from a week's honeymoon in Crikvenica. Anita had been on the original holiday there, and they both now planned to train for full-time work with the church. The church had, indeed, been a place of rest and support for them in 1994, as their parents had been opposed their marriage.

That same Sunday evening service, Jasna, too, arrived from a three-day trip into east Mostar. Nikola, Sandra and many other members of the church had been anxious all day for Jasna's safe return. They were relieved to see her arrive during the evening meeting and eager to hear what she had discovered and experienced.

'It was so sad,' she said afterwards, 'to see the way the city now is. As Muslims, it could so easily have been Tibor and me trapped there, in east Mostar. My roots are there, in the east. I used to paint over there. Now we should have a church there.'

It was Jasna who located Alesa and his family, passing the note of their address to Nikola. She had been responsible, it seemed a lifetime ago, for getting copies of *Peace With God* into the prison, and she had introduced Alesa to the church. In the April of 1994, in more dangerous conditions, she had smuggled Tibor briefly into the east. Now, the time was right for the church, counting Muslim converts already among its strongest members, to play its part in east Mostar. Nikola wondered whether Jasna might become the first missionary to be sent out from the Mostar church.

Newborn children, welcomed and loved by the church; young people who had met and married through youth work and who were now offering themselves as leaders for the future; tears in worship, as people who had suffered loss overflowed not with bitterness but with gratitude and joy; laughter, cheers, applause as Christians from every ethnic group affirmed, together, their community; recent converts praying, and working, towards mission; an architect's drawings for a unique new centre—all these were the threads and currents of a growing, living church in Mostar.

If any one word were chosen to sum up the role of Mostar's church, it would be hope. When Nikola and Sandra drove, in sombre silence, the few kilometres from Mostar to Citluk, abandoning the city to its second war, it was hope that made them turn around. They knew, in the midst of desperate fear, that hope could make a difference. Just to be there, just to hold on to hope, when others had lost it, was enough. It was hope that brought new life to Janos and Razija, and to Jasna and Tibor; it was hope that kept Irena and Gabriel strong in an overcrowded prison; and it was hope that sustained Esad and Zvjezdana when it was possible that their daughter was dying.

It is hope, today, that restores emotions, and brings *melem* to the souls of young and old alike, giving them back a future. The church in Mostar, the charity Novi Most, and the planned new judo club, have grown from the same seed, planted by a couple who dared to believe that hope could be stronger than war.

The consultation document 'Hope For Europe', published jointly by the European Evangelical Alliance and the Lausanne Europe Committee, says:

Millions of our fellow Europeans face an uncertain and sombre future, despite the overthrow of dictators and the passing of the Cold War. Christians have a word of hope for modern Europeans that no one else can speak.

In all Europe, no one has been asked to face as uncertain and sombre a future as have the people of the former Republic of Yugoslavia, and particularly of Bosnia, during 1993 and 1994. A report published by Moj Bliznji in late 1994 provides the appalling toll of the war:

More than 200,000 people have died since the war broke out. Over 1,000,000 people have been wounded or crippled; many are also suffering from psychological trauma. More than 4,000,000 have been forced to leave their homes. Many have been eye-witnesses to the killing of their families. Every individual has been affected, in one way or another, by these atrocities.

Christians do have words of hope for Europe—and the Christians of Mostar have been bold enough to speak it. Hope is the pillar on which their church has been modelled.

It will be years, perhaps generations, before the echoes of war die out in Mostar. Emilija Jupek put it this way:

'I think it will be all right in fifty years. We used to hear of partisans fighting the Germans. Now we are friends with the Germans—but it took fifty years to change.'

In some lives, the hatred and distrust will never go. For the church, the work will be as long and hard in peace as it has been in war. For years to come, it will still be picking up the pieces. But there is, always, hope. A violent divorce has ripped Bosnia apart as painfully as it would a family, leaving emotional as well as physical wounds. But reconciliation is possible, and the birth of a new church family shows it. The Christian faith has brought *melem* to the open wounds of Mostar.

What difference did it make, then, that Nikola and Sandra turned back, in Citluk, to Mostar?

Stevo Dereta has faced the question many times.

'It was difficult for us, we were too far away', he says. 'Moj Bliznji is not such a big organization that it can stretch so easily beyond its circle of influence. Sometimes my people complained. They asked: "Why do we work so much for Mostar?" I said, "Maybe we don't see now, but wait, you will see." I was only afraid that Nikola and Sandra would not be able to hold such a burden, that it would be too much for them. But what God has done through them is wonderful. Mostar is a gate for Bosnia. Christian soldiers' feet are there.'

Epilogue

Paul Brooks, UK Director of Novi Most, dialled Sandra and Nikola's number in Mostar for the 56th time in five days. For months, the main telephone trunk line into Mostar, linking the city to the outside world, had been little more than a cable thrown, unprotected, along the roadside. Was the line now broken?

Sandra's message had been left at the Novi Most office over the weekend: she needed urgently to talk to Paul about a new development in their work. Finally, at the 56th attempt, the call went through. For Paul, it opened a new chapter in the Novi Most story. For the first time, mention was made of the city of Tuzla.

TUZLA, NORTH-EAST BOSNIA, OCTOBER 1994

A few days before, Karmelo Kresonja and Nikola viewed the city of Tuzla from the mountain road. Unable to use the main routes north and east from Mostar, and blocked off by the siege of Sarajevo, they had climbed into the hills in their four-wheel-drive Jeep, along roads that most other vehicles could not use.

Three weeks earlier, after a minor traffic incident in Mostar, they had almost lost the vehicle. A local criminal, armed with a Kalashnikov gun, had fired warning shots towards Karmelo, forcing him to stop and hand over the keys. Even when the police recovered the vehicle, it was kept impounded until the keys, too, were recovered. Now, just days into its freedom, it was fulfilling an essential task.

Nikola and Karmelo had come to Tuzla in response to a cry for help. Seventy-five kilometres north-east of Sarajevo, Tuzla was isolated and its people were hungry. Only fifty kilometres from the border with Croatia, it was cut off from help by a thin wedge of the Krajina crescent: Serb-held territory that could not be crossed. The only route open came from Mostar, over tortuous roads which were all but impassable in winter. Food supplies in the city had dwindled and only a trickle of aid now came in. The Muslim population were weak for lack of food. Some would die within weeks unless a greater flow of supplies could be established.

In Tuzla, Nikola and Karmelo had found workers ready and willing to help, potential premises for a warehouse and office, and an apartment for a worker. It was Nikola's report of the trip to Sandra that initiated her call to the United Kingdom—a desperate plea, once more, for funds and help. The Christians of Mostar, in the youngest church in the Balkans, had begun to see themselves not only as receivers but as givers; the mission church was becoming the sending church. Already, by the time Sandra spoke to Paul, Klaus Domke had volunteered to move up to Tuzla, to co-ordinate the distribution of incoming aid. A four-wheel-drive truck was now needed to cross the mountains, along with increased aid to Mostar, of which part could be redirected.

'I believe that Tuzla is strategic for the church,' Nikola said, 'but that is not our motivation. Church or no church, we have a duty to tell the world what is happening in Tuzla, and to do everything we can to stop people dying this winter.'

Two years earlier, Stevo Dereta and Peter Mackenzie had returned from a similar trip, not to Tuzla, but to Sarajevo, via Mostar. They had brought out the same message. 'When winter comes,' Stevo had repeated over and over, 'people will die.'

Then, it had been Nikola who heard the cry for help. Inexperienced, alone and afraid, he went to Mostar. Now, it is Nikola and Sandra, the experienced church leaders and aid workers, who bring the reports and Klaus, the young German, who agrees to go. Without the first response, there would be no one to make the second. Obedience, and the willingness to go, make possible the obedience and willingness of others. Courage breeds courage. Hope spreads, like a gentle wave, passed on one to one.

Acknowledgments

Quotation from 'Holocaust and Ethnic Cleansing' by Philip Yancey used by permission of *Christianity Today, 1993*

Quotation from 'Summer Holiday' words and music by Bruce Welch and Brian Bennett
© 1963 Reproduced by permission of EMI Music Publishing Ltd trading as Elstree Music, London WC2H OEA

Quotation from 'Honeymoon Flight' in *Death of a Naturalist* by Seamus Heaney used by permission of Faber and Faber Ltd

Quotation from the dedication of *Homeland* by Stewart Henderson used by permission of Hodder and Stoughton Ltd

Quotation from 'Gun' in *The King of Twist*, by Steve Turner, used by permission of Hodder and Stoughton Ltd

Quotation from 'Liturgy' in *Rebel Without Applause* by Gerard Kelly © 1991 Kingsway

Quotation from *Hope for the World* by Jon Birch used by permission of Serious Music UK